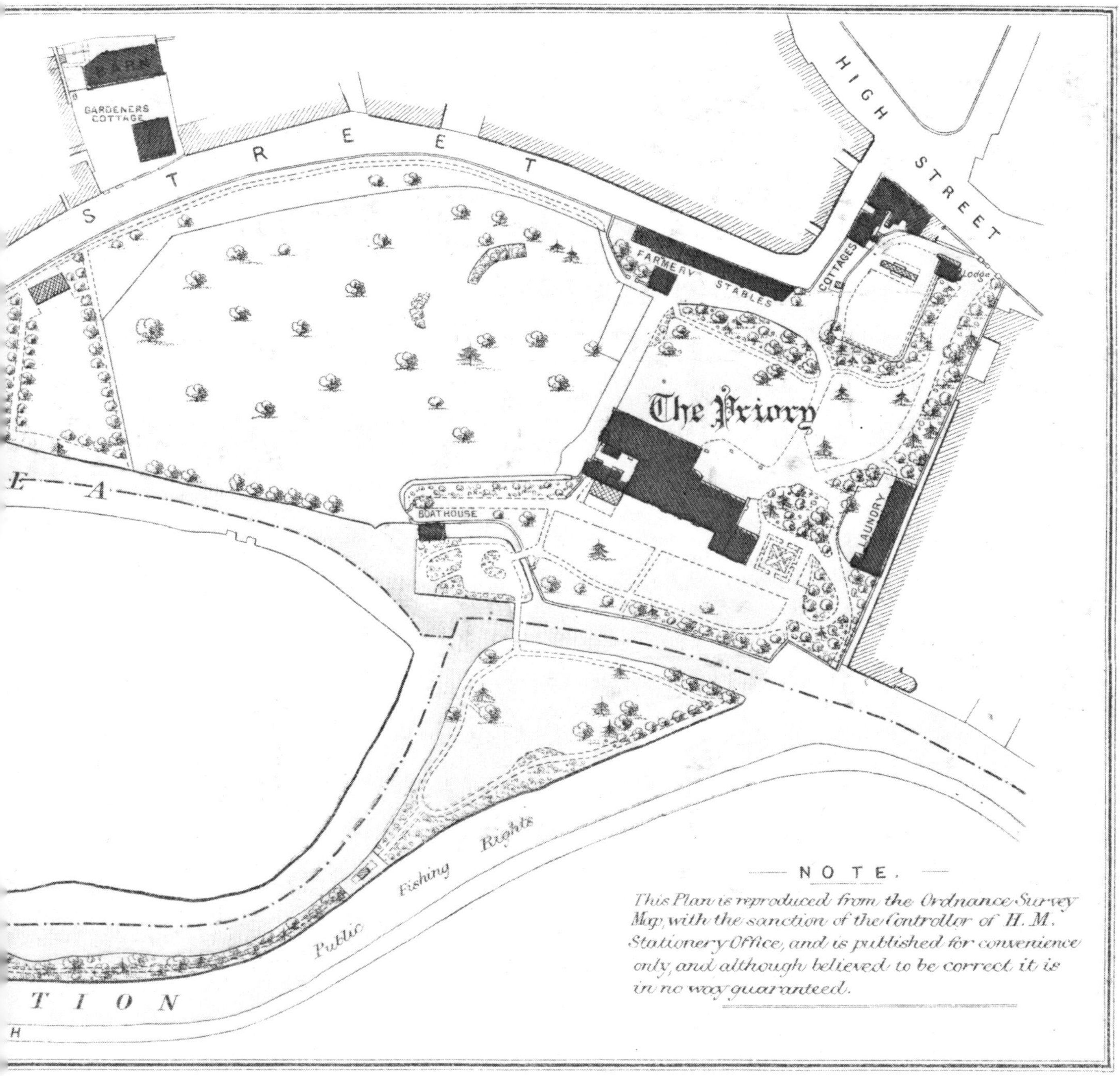

BARN

GARDENERS COTTAGE

STREET

HIGH STREET

FARMERY

STABLES

COTTAGES

Lodge

The Priory

BOATHOUSE

LAUNDRY

E A

TION

H

Public Fishing Rights

NOTE.

This Plan is reproduced from the Ordnance Survey Map, with the sanction of the Controller of H. M. Stationery Office, and is published for convenience only, and although believed to be correct it is in no way guaranteed.

The Book of Ware 1977
has been published as a
Limited Edition of which
this is

Number 625

A complete list of the
original subscribers is
printed at the back of
the book

THE BOOK OF WARE

FRONT COVER: John Gilpin's ride—from 19th c.,stained glass at Amwell House.

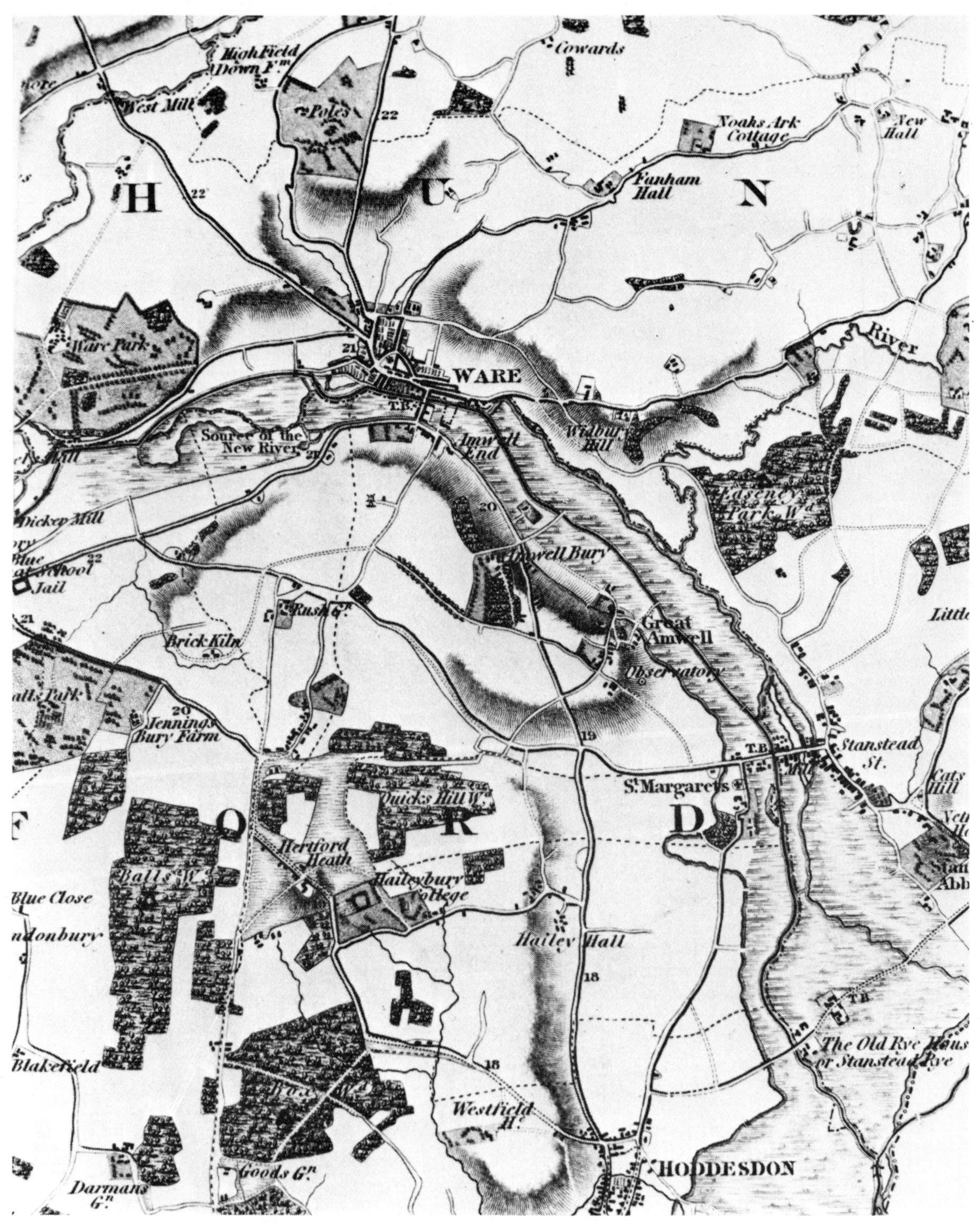

An 1822 map of Ware and Great Amwell with their environs. A large part of the area to the left of the River Lee was in the ecclesiastical parish of Great Amwell.

THE BOOK OF WARE

A PORTRAIT OF THE TOWN

BY

CYRIL HEATH

BARRACUDA BOOKS LIMITED
CHESHAM, BUCKINGHAMSHIRE, ENGLAND
MCMLXXVII

PUBLISHED BY BARRACUDA BOOKS LIMITED

CHESHAM, ENGLAND

AND PRINTED BY

FRANK ROOK LIMITED

TOWER BRIDGE ROAD

LONDON SE1

BOUND BY

BOOKBINDERS OF LONDON LIMITED

LONDON N5

JACKET PRINTED BY

WHITE CRESCENT PRESS LIMITED

LUTON, ENGLAND

LITHOGRAPHY BY

SOUTH MIDLANDS LITHO PLATES LIMITED

LUTON, ENGLAND

TYPE SET IN

MONOTYPE BASKERVILLE SERIES 169

BY SOUTH BUCKS TYPESETTERS LIMITED

BEACONSFIELD, ENGLAND

ISBN 0 86023 035 X

Contents

Acknowledgements

This is a book which has been written as much by the people of Ware as by me. The support and help I have had has been magnificent, and on occasions from the most unexpected quarter.

From the very first Sir John Hanbury, himself keenly interested in the history of the area, has helped and guided me, and County Councillor Charles Bowsher has been a most enthusiastic supporter.

The sources of the town's history have always been available from county archives, with particular help from Miss Eileen Lynch. Hertford Museum too has helped considerably through the curator, Gordon Davies, and his assistant, Mrs Liz Barratt. The Victoria and Albert Museum provided up-to-date information on the Bed of Ware.

The county library has offered encouragement, and especially the staffs at the Ware and Hertford branches in assisting with the subscription lists.

The Mayor of Ware, Cllr John Bishop and his wife, have helped tremendously, and town clerk, C. H. Humphreys, has gone out of his way to be of assistance.

The Chamber of Trade has been most enthusiastic in its help, so too has Ware College of Further Education through the head of Liberal Studies, Eric Wilson, and head of the photographic department, Paul Damen, who provided many of the modern pictures.

Main burden of the historic pictures fell on Mike Poultney, and he has produced prints of a very high standard. Mike Glue took the aerial picture of the town centre from a balloon, and Michael Evans provided me with some excellent prints.

Tim Chaplin loaned me three unique picture albums dating between 1891 and 1895 from which I was able to take several prints.

Clive Partridge, Director of 'Rescue' Excavations in East Herts, gave me invaluable help on the Genesis chapter, and I had a lot of help from the Wren Library at Trinity College, Cambridge.

Allen & Hanburys Ltd., gave permission for several pictures to be used from the book 'Through a City Archway', and L. G. Ford, of D. Wickham and Co., was most helpful too.

Valuable information on Christ Church was supplied by R. Boutell, and the Sisters at the Carmelite Monastery at Ware Park showed a lively interest. The Rev C. E. C. Walker, Vicar of St John the Baptist, Great Amwell, was a great help, and Mrs Ella Way and W. J. Page provided a large collection of old postcards, some of which have been used.

Brig R. L. Allen helped on the Fanhams Hall pictures, and Eric Porteous with information about the old gas works.

But this has been a combined effort, and my thanks go to the many people who wrote, telephoned, or contacted me personally with helpful suggestions.

Foreword

by Sir John Hanbury

The town with which this book is concerned is spectacular neither in its setting nor its architecture, but its roots are as deep in history and pre-history as any in England. Geologists say that some thousands of years ago the Lea Valley was indeed the valley of the Thames also as it made its way eastwards to join the Rhine in the middle of what is now the North Sea. Ware is set at a narrowing of the otherwise wide and marshy valley and has from time immemorial been an important crossing point of this natural obstacle. The earliest evidence of human occupation is the Iron Age settlement on the hill to the north of the town and when the Romans built Ermine Street, the great road from London to Lincoln and York, it crossed the valley here on a combination of causeway and bridge. Later the Danish invaders were able to bring their sea-going ships right up to Ware and it is probable that Harold's army passed nearby on its way to challenge the Normans in 1066. The town also figured in the campaigns of the Wars of the Roses and in the Civil War of Cromwell's time, so that its fine old church and Priory and the many old houses in its High Street have seen history being unfolded before them. Surely the doings of the people who saw and participated in these events and the buildings that they left behind them are worthy to be recorded for posterity, that we may be inspired to preserve and emulate all that is best in the legacy that our forebears have passed down to us.

AMWELLBURY,
GT AMWELL.
February, 1977

John Hanbury.

Preface

by Charles Bowsher, Hertfordshire County Councillor, and First Town Mayor of Ware

Every present, former or future resident of Ware will wish to read and own this book. It will certainly enhance the sincere belief that so many hold of belonging, and being part of the Community in which we live.

I envy Cyril Heath his energy, dedication and patience in undertaking this work. I cannot imagine any task more satisfying than the completion of such an absorbingly difficult endeavour. My personal gratitude to him for his enterprise in embarking on this second chronicle is certain to be shared by all local citizens.

I hope this book is the great success it deserves to be, and I am sure it would have met with the instant approval of the late Edith Hunt, a former local historian. I commend it in the conviction that the reader will be both entertained and enlightened by The Book of Ware.

Charles Bowsher.

The Bed of Ware

Sir Toby Belch: Go, write it in a martial
hand; be curst and brief; it is
no matter how witty, so it be
eloquent and full of invention;
taunt him with the licence of ink;
if thou 'thou'st' him some thrice,
it shall not be amiss; and as many lies
as will lie in thy sheet of paper,
although the sheet were big enough
for the bed of Ware in England, set
'em down. . . .
Shakespeare's *Twelfth Night*, first
performed 1601.

The Great Bed of Ware. (Photo: Sally Chappell).

Cave

The Latin motto on the town coat of arms—adopted in the 1960s—is a mystery to some townspeople. Was someone trying to issue a warning against outsiders—or neighbours?

Cave means Beware, and the town could not very well be anything else! Yes, when the coat of arms was adopted in the 1960s, no less a body than the College of Heralds suggested the motto, and intended it as yet another pun on the town's name.

It could, however, have been a warning to anyone delving into the town's history. All is not what it seems. A Priory, which was never a Priory; a Manor House which was never a Manor House, and relics and documents which seem to be scattered in many strange places.

Like it or not, much of Ware's history is intertwined with near neighbour Hertford, and as an example, the story of the 1241 tournament on the Meads, when the Earl of Pembroke was killed, is claimed by both towns, and contemporary records do not help.

This is not a definitive history. The scholar can dig deeper by making use of the Bibliography at the back of the book. For those who are just curious about the town's history this is a selection of items which interested me. Many of the pictures have never been published before.

There is a need in the area for a repository for items from the past. Many items of interest to Ware are in private hands, and this applies to Bishop's Stortford too. The ideal plan would be to turn Hertford Museum into an East Herts Museum, with small exhibitions in the larger centres. The growing interest in our forefathers should be fostered and developed, but, alas, too often this sort of activity comes at the bottom of the list of priorities.

CAVE

The town crest of Ware

ABOVE: One of the earliest resting places of the Great Bed of Ware, The George Inn. The print is earlier than 1760. The inn stood on the site now occupied by Barclay's Bank Ltd., in High Street. It was Isaac Walton who referred to a picture of a great trout at 'Mine Host Rickabie's', at The George.

LEFT: The Great Bed of Ware, drawn in 1832 when it rested at the Saracens Head in High Street, and RIGHT: The Saracens Head in High Street, its last resting place in the town *c*1920. The public house was demolished, and a modern, river-side hostelry has replaced it.

Ware Four

Ware is known nationally on four counts, three of which are light-hearted; the fourth—perhaps not so well known—resulted in disaster.

The name of the town lends itself to the most excruciating puns, which, after using the chapter heading as an example, are best left alone.

It is the Bed of Ware which has probably brought the town the greatest publicity, and modern research suggests it was built for that reason.

Peter Thornton, Keeper of Furniture and Woodwork at the Victoria and Albert Museum, where the great bed now is, in a booklet published in 1977, says: 'Defaced, altered, and shorn of its hangings, the Great Bed of Ware is still an impressive object. It probably represents the best of indigenous craftsmanship in wood of the Elizabethan period, but its fame rested from the outset on its enormous size rather than on any aesthetic merits it may have. And its fame has ensured that its name is woven into the very fabric of English history.'

The mattress is nine feet square, while the bed is 10ft 7ins wide, 10ft 10ins long, and 8ft 9ins high. Fable has it that the bed was built in 1463 by Jonas Fosbrooke, having taken him 30 years to make, and presented to Edward IV for royal use on state occasions. The date was painted on the headboard.

For many years it was widely accepted that it was originally installed at Ware Manor, but that Thomas Fanshawe, when he moved his manor to Ware Park, discarded the bed, which was snapped up by one of the large inns in the town.

Mr Thornton, having examined the workmanship, says it could not have been made much before 1590, and it was certainly well-known to Shakespeare, who mentions it in *Twelfth Night*, first performed in 1601.

Professional opinion suggests it was not made for a manor house, because the workmanship is not of the high order expected for a grand house, and Mr Thornton is convinced that it was built as what we would now call 'an advertising gimmick'.

If it was, then it succeeded, as Sir Toby Belch said in *Twelfth Night*. In 1609 Ben Jonson referred to it in his play *Epicone*; or the Silent Woman. Daw says 'Why, we have been . . . ' La-Foole: 'In the great bed of Ware together in our time.'

And in 1706 George Farquhar mentions it in his play *The Recruiting Officer*—'A mighty large bed, bigger by half than the great bed of Ware. Ten thousand people may be in it together and never feel one another'. Byron mentions it in *Don Juan*, written between 1817 and 1820, and Vallans brings it into the *Tale of Two Swannes*, written about 1589.

In 1610 Prince Ludwig Friedrich of Wurttemberg stayed a night at Ware, and slept in a bed 'eight feet wide'. His secretary said he stayed at 'The Stag', but it must have been the White Hart.

It remained there until 1706 when it was transferred to The George. It then moved to The Crown, the principal inn in Ware, which was demolished in 1765. The bed then went to the Saracens Head, which was demolished in the late 1950s, and a new inn was built on the riverside by the bridge.

The bed was used for lodging soldiers in 1765, and one militiaman carved his name and the date 1761 on the woodwork. Many other people have done the same.

On one occasion six citizens and their wives came from London 'in a frolic to sport themselves'. Having dined exceedingly well, they went up to sleep in the great bed. They worked out a cunning way whereby they could all lie in the bed without unduly disturbing each other, but mine host had other plans for them. He laced their nightcap with a powder which had such disastrous effect that 'they departed hastily back to London'.

The bed was purchased from the Saracens Head for 100 gns in 1870, and although the story went that it had been bought by a Hertford man for Charles Dickens, it ended up at Rye House Hotel, Hoddesdon, where the owner built a special building in the garden to house it, and other antiquities he had collected.

After passing into the hands of the brewers, it was eventually secured by Messrs Frank Partridge & Co., in 1931, and purchased by the Victoria and Albert Museum for £4,000, half of which was contributed by the National Art Collection Fund.

The bed featured at the Theatre Royal in 1839, when a play, *The Merrie Devil of Edmonton—or The Great Bed of Ware* was presented. A large replica of the bed was used in the fifth scene.

Almost from the start, there used to hang a large set of antlers in the same room as the bed, and a custom grew that the innkeeper, for a fee, proclaimed a cautionary oath over the visitors. It went as follows:

'Take care thou'st thy self no wrong;
Drink no small beer if thou hast strong;
And farther do thyself this Right,
Eat no Brown Bread if thou hast white;
And if the Mistress thou canst Bed
Be sure thou dost not Kiss the Maid.
Show not thy Wife thy utmost Strength,
Nor let her know the Purses length;
Never be bound for any Friend,
But rather far thy Money lend;
For thou wilt find 'tis better he
Should break or be undone than thee;

Trust no Man that is Proud and Poor,
Unless thou wilt forgive the Score;
For he will never pay or own
The Kindness thou to him hast shown;
Be just and Grateful to thy Friend
'Twill make thee happy in the end;
But if thyself and thine Thou'dst save,
Take care thou dealst not with a Knave;
Trust not thy Wife, tho' ne'er so good,
With no Man but thyself Abroad.
For if thou do'st, e'er she returns,
Thy forehead may be deck'd with Horns:
What I have said do thou retain,
So kiss the Horns and say, Amen.'

The White Hart was one of the oldest and most important of Ware inns, and stood on ground now occupied by Nos. 75, 77 and 79 High Street. The Crown was on the site of 87 High Street, and The George stood on the site of Barclay's Bank Ltd., in High Street, and over 27 and 31 High Street. The three hotels were large and had, over the years, many important guests.

There was a fourth inn which was an important part of the town, The Bull, which appropriately stood on the site of the present Post Office. When Ware became a post town in 1536, it was to The Bull that the post came, and there the horses were changed.

Mr James Smith, a former Ware man who lived in Australia wrote a long description of the Ware of his childhood, in the early 1800s: 'Upwards of twenty York and Cambridge coaches—some of them famous for their speed—changed horses at the Bull.'

Ware's third claim to national fame is the famous ride of John Gilpin immortalised by the poet William Cowper in the early 1780s. The full title is *The Diverting History of John Gilpin; showing how he went farther than he intended, and came safe home again.*

His wife, according to the poem, reminded him that they had been married 20 years and had arranged to go on the following day for a celebration to the Bell at Edmonton, not far from their home. The family were to go in a chaise and pair, with Gilpin following on a horse borrowed from a friend, who was a calender—a man who pressed cloth.

All went well until, with the bottles of wine strapped to his back, the horse bolted, and the luckless Gilpin could not stop it until it got to Ware, where its owner lived. As the horse flew past the Bell at Edmonton, Gilpin's wife told him he had arrived:

But yet his horse was not a whit
Inclined to tarry there;
For why? his owner had a house
Full ten miles off, at Ware.

Most people have believed the story to be fictional, but the Rev Robert Aris Willmott, in his book published in 1850 describes how the poem was written. It appears that a friend, Lady Austen was part of the poet's evening circle, and on one occasion saw him sinking into increasing dejection.

'It was her custom, on these occasions, to try all the resources of her sprightly powers for his immediate relief. She told him the story of John Gilpin (which had been treasured in her memory from her childhood), to dissipate the gloom of the passing hour.'

Cowper told her the next morning that 'convulsions of laughter' brought on by his recollection of her story had kept him awake during the greater part of the night, and that he had turned it into a ballad.

Ware's fourth adventure into national history, perhaps not so well known, is that it was in the town that Lady Jane Grey was proclaimed Queen of England on 14 July, 1553.

Lady Jane was the eldest daughter of the Duke and Duchess of Suffolk and a great-neice of Henry VIII. She was born in 1537 and was executed at the age of sixteen and a half. She reigned for nine days between the death of Edward VI and the accession of Mary I.

She was pushed to the throne by William Parr, Marquis of Northampton, and Mary I, on 1 January 1554, indicted him as being a false traitor in arms 'to dispose us of our royal power and kingdom of England on 14 and 15 July, 1 Mary, at our town of Ware in our Co. of Hertford.'

It appears that Northampton had 'assembled to the number of 500 persons in warlike manner at Ware and there falsely and traitorously in writing proclaimed the Duke of Northumberland to be lieutenant general and describing the Queen as the lady Mary the bastard daughter of King Henry VIII and proclaiming at Ware the Lady Jane one of the daughters of the Duke of Suffolk, wife of Guildford Dudley son of the said Duke of Northumberland undoubted Queen. . . .'

Unfortunately for the Duke, however, his forces started to desert him at Ware, and the cause was lost.

ABOVE: Part of the old George Inn went over 31 High Street, pictured today.

BELOW: This coat of arms was found up the chimney of 27 High Street, again part of the George Inn. It was used when James I visited the inn, but put up the chimney and forgotten during Cromwell's Commonwealth.

ABOVE: The modern post office on the site of the old posting inn, The Bull.

BELOW: The modern Saracens Head, with its attractive river-side bars.

LEFT: Lady Jane Grey—by an unknown artist.

RIGHT: The Duke of Northumberland, father-in-law of Lady Jane Grey. As his daughter-in-law was proclaimed Queen at Ware, he was promoted lieutenant-general.

BELOW: John Gilpin on his unrehearsed ride from Edmonton to Ware, A print dated 1801.

ABOVE: A Neolithic polished axe found on the tow path near Ware Lock.

LEFT: When the Beaker folk visited the area between 2000 and 1650 BC, they brought with them some beautiful examples of pottery. This long-necked beaker was found in Watton Road, and RIGHT: This Romano/Saxon pot was found near Ware Lock.

Genesis

In the beginning water covered the earth—and in Ware's case this must have been so. The River Thames once went through the area of the town more than a million years ago, before the Ice Ages. It was in the interval between the second and third Ice Age that the Thames found glacial opposition too much and settled into its present course. After the third Ice Age the Lee cut its way into the Thames, and after the fourth Ice Age, with Britain ceasing to be joined to Europe, and as the glaciers receded, about 7,000 years ago, the Lee and its tributaries were no longer fast flowing waterways, but slowed down. Their valleys then became marshy.

The land was covered by forest, particularly dense south of Ware, and man left only isolated evidence of his passing. Nearly 4,000 years ago, the Beaker Folk left a vessel at Ware, and this fine example of their work is in Hertford Museum. A bronze age site was found on East Herts golf course when the by-pass was cut through.

The Romans left significant traces at Ware lock, rediscovered when it was re-built, and a splendid amphora at Broadmeads, found in 1952. Stone coffins were discovered on Buryfield at the turn of the 19th century, and scattered flints and fragments of early pottery have also been found, but the scale and location of the important Roman river-crossing settlement is still being investigated.

Ermine Street, the Roman road from London to York, crossed the river in the region of Allen and Hanbury's works, and excavations at Ware lock, started in 1974, have concluded that the nucleus of Roman Ware lies somewhere in that area.

The earliest road was 10 metres wide, and was constructed of fairly fine but dirty gravel overlying a layer of peat. The road was later widened, and on the east side there was a pavement of sand. It had V-shaped ditches on either side. These silted rapidly, and the final fourth century road surface spilled out over them. The surface of the road contained many pot-holes and ruts—not unusual features in later Ware roads, as we shall see. Some of these were filled with sand and fine gravel, and one big hole was filled with mortared stones and chalk. A shallow pit contained a cremation burial, and fragments of a pot dateable to the middle of the third century.

Over the shallow silted-up ditches to the west of the road evidence of a building was found. It may have been just a roadside house or shop. Its date—there was evidence of an earlier one on the site—was between 355 and 400. Many of the finds made in Ware in the 19th century seem to have been scattered to the four winds, and cannot be traced. Records of them are not easily found, but in February 1977, ditches of the Iron Age and the Roman periods were found at Buryfields.

Probably before the Romans left, the crossing over the river fell into disrepair and finally ceased to be used. But the town entered history again when the Danes arrived.

The Kingdom of Mercia had extended its boundaries eastwards in the eighth century to the line of Ermine Street, taking in the Western part of the declining Kingdom of the East Saxons. But a Danish invasion had been gathering momentum throughout the ninth century. The Kingdoms of the Saxons and Angles, except Wessex in the south, had been all but wiped out, and their royal families killed. Nearly half the country was in Danish hands by about 878, and King Alfred of Wessex was obliged to divide the country on the line of Watling Street—from Dover to Wroxeter (near Shrewsbury). Alfred counter-attacked, and made the new boundary up the Lee from London, then across to Watling Street, north to Cheshire. Ware was then subject to Danelaw.

Ten years later there was fresh trouble. Another powerful Danish force landed in Kent, led by a veteran Viking, Haesten. This moved into the Thames, thence up the River Lee, and into a situation which, even today, historians cannot agree upon. Some say he set up camp at Ware, and he raided the crops at Hertford, burning what he did not need.

King Alfred certainly decided to do something about it, but what? A popular version is that he went by boat or on horseback down the river, and, finding a place where the opportunity afforded itself, divided the river in three, lowering the waters higher up. The Danes could not sail their ships, and so suffered a crushing defeat. Another story has it that a barrier was placed across the river, which was then tidal, stopping the tide going up.

The only contemporary account is in the Anglo-Saxon Chronicle which says: '894 . . . In the early winter the Danes who were ençamped on Mersea rowed their ships up the Thames and up the Lee. That was two years after they came across the sea.

'895. And in the same year the aforesaid army made a fortress by the Lee, 20 miles above London. Then afterwards in the summer a great part of the citizens and also of other people marched till they arrived at the fortress of the Danes, and they were put to flight and four king's thegns were slain. Then later, in the autumn, the king encamped in the vicinity of the borough (Hertford) while they were reaping their corn, so that the Danes could not deny them that harvest. Then one day the king rode up along the river, and examined where the river could be obstructed, so that they could not bring the ships out. Then they abandoned the ships and went overland till they reached Bridgnorth on the Severn and built that fortress. Then the English rode after the enemy, and the men of London fetched the ships, and broke all which they could not bring away, and brought to London those which were serviceable. And the Danes had placed their women in safety in East Anglia before they left that fortress.'

The defeat is claimed as being at Ware, and at Amwell, whilst there is also a suggestion that it might have been at Stanstead Abbotts.

Because the river fell at Ware, it probably gave rise to the name of the little community. It suggests a corruption of the word weir, which was there, and is now covered by a lock. Some think that there is a missing segment, and it should be Edward's Weir/Ware. Domesday Book adds a final S to the name, and other spellings up to 1200 included Wara, Waer, Warre and Waras.

ABOVE: A late Roman Bowl.

BELOW: A late Roman colour coated beaker, found near Ware Lock.

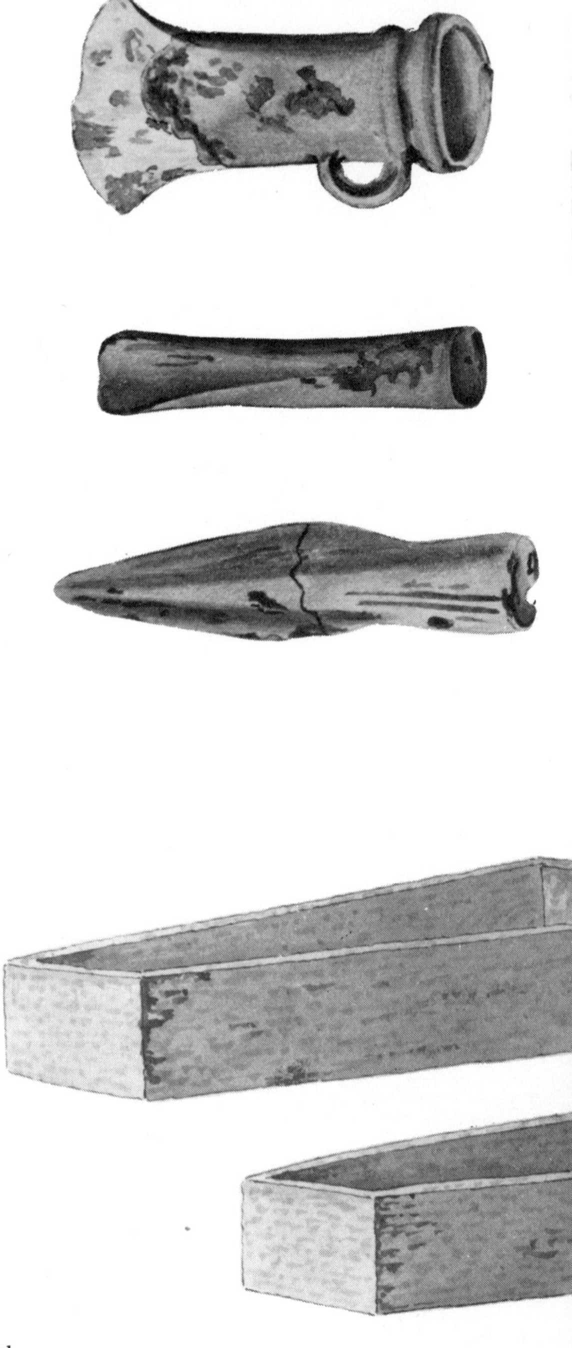

ABOVE: Many of Ware's antiquities discovered in the early 19th century cannot now be found. These drawings of 'antiquities', in the Buckler collection at County Hall, Hertford, were described as having been 'found at a farm near Ware'.

LEFT: This Spanish-type Roman Amphora was found at Broadmeads in 1952. It was used by the Romans for transporting and storing wine and oil. It is now in the town clerk's office at the Priory.

RIGHT: A 13th century greyware pot found at Amwell End.

BELOW: The Buckler collection also contains these drawings of stone coffins 'found in a field near Ware in 1802'. In all there were four. Some had bones and small lumps of brass in them, and some had 'warlike weapons'. One coffin had a coin on it, and in another the skeleton looked as if it had been 'bedded in white powder'. No one knows where the coffins or the relics are today.

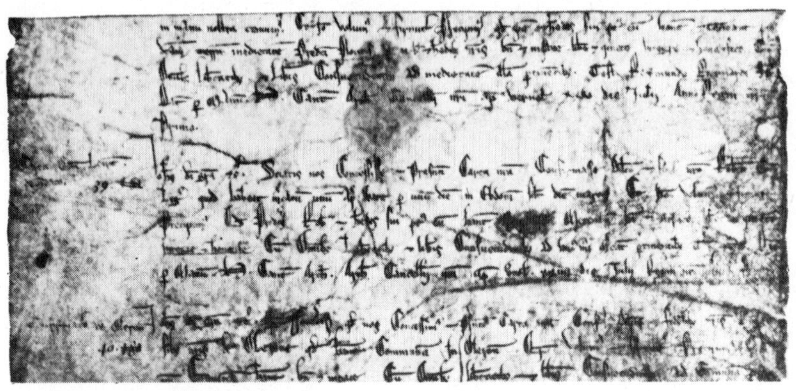

ABOVE: King John granted a market to the Earl of Leicester on July 24th, 1199. This is part of the charter. The market was to be held at Ware on a Tuesday—market day is still on a Tuesday. The charter was probably granted because the Earl was a steward at the king's coronation. It was witnessed by Hubert, Archbishop of Canterbury.

BELOW: This is part of the charter, dated March 10th, 1207 which granted to Petronilla, Countess of Leicester, toll on goods going down the river. The Sheriff of Hertford and his bailiffs were ordered 'not to disturb her'.

Man Maketh Manors

First real documentary evidence of the town of Ware lies in the Domesday Book of 1086. It runs thus: 'Hugh de Grentmaisnil holds in Waras 24 hides. There is land for 38 ploughs. In the desmesne there are 13 hides and on it are 3 ploughs. There could be 3 more. There are 38 villeins and a priest and the reeve of the vill and 3 Frenchmen and 2 Englishmen have 26 ploughs and a half-plough. There are 27 bordars and 12 cottars and 9 serfs. Under the Frenchmen and the Englishmen are 32 men between villeins and bordars. There are 2 mills worth 24 shillings and 400 eels less 25 and other men have 3 mills producing 10s yearly. Meadow is there sufficient for 20 plough teams, woodland to feed 400 swine. There is an enclosure for beasts of the chase and 4 arpents of vineyard just planted. The total value is 45 pounds, when received it was 50 pounds. This manor Anschil of Waras held and 1 Sokeman, his man, had there 2 hides and another sokeman, earl Guert's man held half a hide. Either could sell. These two, after King William came, were attached to this manor. They did not belong to it in King Edward's time, so the shire moot testifies.'

From this it can be estimated that the population was substantial for the time. The 'enclosure for beasts of the chase', and the vineyards were in the area of what is now known as Ware Park.

Lord of the Manor, Hugh de Grentmaisnil, was a military strategist, and had helped William plan his invasion of this country. A grateful monarch presented him with the lands, rights and obligations which made up the manor, although there is no record of the unfortunate previous owner.

However, it is known that Grentmaisnil was not the first Norman owner. This was Ralf Taillebois who, after two years, swapped the land for some in Bedfordshire.

Hugh's son, Ivo, disgraced himself and his family in some way which history does not record, and thus did not inherit the manor. In 1173 it was certainly in the hands of King Henry II, but the lands reverted to the family again through Parnel, or Petronil, Hugh's daughter, who married Robert Earl of Leicester.

In 1190 their second son, Robert Fitz Parnel, succeeded to the property, and he obtained a grant for a weekly market in Ware in 1199, no doubt for service to King John in acting as steward at his coronation.

But Robert did not live long, dying in 1207, and his mother held the manor in dower until 1212. Then Sayer de Quencey, Earl of Winchester, husband of her daughter Margaret, became lord of the manor.

Ware had had problems ever since the Conquest because its affairs had been placed under the Bailiff of Hertford, who favoured his own town at the expense of Ware. In the name of the King he claimed monopoly of the highways, trying to block Ware ford and chain the bridge, so that all traffic went through Hertford, which could claim the tolls.

It became such a lively issue that in 1191 the men of Hertford went to Ware and broke down the bridge. In Sayer de Quencey, Ware had a great champion. He was in opposition to King John from the first, being Justiciar of England from 1211-14. But he chose his moment to free Ware from the attentions of the Bailiff of Hertford.

With Hertford Castle beseiged by the Dauphin of France and his troops, de Quencey thought the bailiff would have too much on his mind to notice that the iron bars across Ware bridge had been broken, and the chain across the ford thrown into the river.

Not content with that, de Quencey sent a message to the Bailiff saying that he would follow the chain if he wanted to make anything of it.

The Bailiff, more concerned for his own neck at the time, left well alone, and although there were various later attempts to re-assert Hertford's authority over Ware, they were generally doomed to failure. De Quencey died on a Crusade, and his widow, Margaret took his mantle, although she spent much of her time at the Alien Benedictine Priory.

Illegal market days formed Hertford's next complaint. It appears these were held in the same day as those at Hertford; also 'that the lady and bailiff of Ware held fairs in the town of Ware twice in September.' Hertford burgesses also complained that never before the war between King John and the Barons used any cart to cross at Ware bridge.

They added: 'There used to be a certain bar closed and near the bridge there used to be a certain iron chain'. More complaints—'Before the Barons War no dyers, weavers or tanners in vill of Ware, but after there were dyers and weavers but no tanners.' But they did nothing about it, and evidently no one took any notice of them.

Margaret died in 1235, and was succeeded by Roger de Quencey, and six years later a contentious tournament was held. Some authorities say it was at Ware, some at Hertford. The most contemporary document says it was held a 'bowshot from Hertford.'

Tournaments were banned by the Pope, but this was organised by Gilbert Marshal, Earl of Pembroke. The Earl rode a horse to which he was unused, and when the trumpets blew, calling the knights to the lists, his horse unseated him, galloping off across the meads.

The unfortunate knight was unable to get his mail-clad foot free and was dragged along with the horse. He later died in Hertford Priory, and there then started a wrangle as to where he should be buried. A compromise was reached whereby his heart and entrails were buried at the priory church, and his body in the Temple Church in London.

Nichols' History of Leicester tells of a tournament in Ware in 1276, when Ernald de Bois, of Weston-in-Arden was killed.

Roger granted the tenancy of the manor to his brother Robert in 1253, but he died in 1257. He served Henry III in the wars in France, and at Bordeaux in 1254, the king granted a licence for an annual fair to be held 'on the eve and day of the Nativity of the Virgin Mary and the three days following.' This fair continued for almost 700 years, but was discontinued in 1936 because there was no ground available for it.

After the death of Robert de Quencey, the manor was held for a period by Roger's three daughters: Margaret, wife of William Ferrers, fifth Earl of Derby; Elizabeth, or Isabel, wife of Alexander Comyn, Earl of Buchan, and Helen, or Ela, wife of Alan la Zouche of Ashby-de-la-Zouche. Eventually the whole manor became Margaret's and she gave it to her second son William.

But the Ferrers appeared to have had very little to do with the manor, which was tenanted by Joan, Robert de Quencey's elder daughter. Joan de Bohun lived at the Benedictine Priory and made additions to the buildings, but they were knocked down by the Prior as soon as she died. The manor then passed to her sister, Hawise, the widow of Baldwin Wake. Her son, John, succeeded as a minor in the custody of Queen Eleanor in 1285. He did homage for the lands in 1290, but died in 1300.

During the minority of the heir, Thomas Wake, the manor was assigned in 1310, to William Trente for three years. This discharged a debt due to him for wine from the King's butler, Henry de Say. But in 1338, Thomas gave land in Ware for the establishment of a Franciscan Friary, and more land was given by his widow, Blanche, in 1349. At about the time that Edward II's mother, Queen Isabella stayed at Hertford Castle, Thomas was its custodian.

His sister, Margaret, was married to Edmund, Earl of Kent, youngest son of Edward I. Widowed, she inherited the manor from her brother, but she too died in the year of the Black Death, 1349. Her second son, John, succeeded her, but he too died three years later, and the manor passed to his heiress, Joan.

Joan, the wife of Thomas de Holand, Earl of Kent, was known as the Fair Maid of Kent. Her second marriage was to Edward, the Black Prince, and she was the mother of King Richard II. Tradition has it that Lady Joan had some interest in the building of St Mary's Church. Her badge can certainly be seen in both the north and south aisles.

After her death in 1385 the manor went to her son by the Earl of Kent, but he died in 1397. In turn he was succeeded by his son—Thomas, Earl of Kent—but he did not hold the manor for long either. After being created Earl of Surrey, he was imprisoned and later beheaded at Cirencester in 1399, for reasons which appear to have been connected with his sympathies for Richard II. His lands were forfeited to Henry IV.

The manor was later restored to Edmund, Earl of Kent, brother and heir to Thomas, but he died in 1408. His sister, Alianore, wife of Thomas Montagu, Earl of Salisbury, inherited the manor, and her husband is said to have presented the font to the church.

But soon the manor was to become crown property again. The Earl of Salisbury's daughter, Alice, married Sir Richard Neville, and it was their son Richard, Earl of Warwick (known as the Kingmaker), who later held it. He was killed at the battle of Barnet in 1471, but his daughter, Anne, married into royalty.

Her first husband was Edward, Prince of Wales, who was killed after the battle of Tewkesbury, and then Richard, Duke of Gloucester, who became king in 1483. With the manor crown property, in 1485 Sir Robert Brackenbury, Constable of the Tower, was appointed steward, with fees of £5 a year.

Queen Anne died in 1485 and her nephew, Edward Earl of Warwick succeeded to her property, but he did not hold Ware. Henry VII granted the property to his mother, Margaret, Countess of Richmond. It is again part of the town tradition that Gilpin House, in the High Street, and now a furniture shop, was built by Henry VII for his mother.

When she died in 1509, Sir Thomas Lovell, treasurer of the household, was given charge of the manor, and a year later William Compton, groom of the state, became bailiff of both town and manor, keeper of the park, meadows, fishery, and two mills.

But the vagaries of the times overtook Ware again. In 1513, Lady Margaret Pole, sister and heiress of Edward Plantagenet, Earl of Warwick, was reinstated as Countess of Salisbury, and Ware manor was restored to her.

Henry VIII was jealous of her, however, and was suspicious of the fact that she was a member of the old royal household. As was Henry's way with people who appeared to be in his way, he had her beheaded in 1541.

Once again Ware was held by the crown, and in 1542 Thomas Wrothe was appointed bailiff and keeper of the park etc, and John Noode was granted the fishery—worth, by the way £7 a year, and let for about £3.70 a year. The two corn mills were leased to Thomas Lennard for 40 years.

Six years later Edward VI granted the estate to his sister Mary, but when she became Queen in 1553, it was handed to Francis, Earl of Huntingdon and his wife Katherine. By then it consisted of the manor, park and three mills. The transfer was confirmed by Elizabeth I in 1570, but she cut out the park, mills and fishery.

But the Huntingdons were deeply in debt, and in 1575 they sold up to Mr Thomas Fanshawe, the Queen's Remembrancer, who acquired the entire property, and revived all the rights of the lord of the manor. Thomas certainly made his mark on the town, and was soon claiming fines paid at the sessions—because his tenants charged too much for beer. Changes were also in the offing, and Thomas started to build himself a new manor house in Ware Park, keeping the old building as a dower house.

Thomas died in 1601, and was succeeded by his son Henry. He too followed in the office of King's Remembrancer, but was also a noted horticulturist. The gardens at Ware Park were fine indeed, and the king was so pleased with the grapes and peaches that he sent for them twice a week.

Sir Henry—he was knighted in 1603—had trouble with the Ware people, and castigated them for using a recreation field without leave. He also brought a suit against one Henry Obaston for ploughing up part of Berry Close (now Buryfield—and not as is popularly believed, a place where London plague victims were interred). The close ground was used for the mustering of trained bands. Sir Henry died in 1615, and his son Thomas succeeded him.

Thomas and his brother Richard played a great part in the Civil War, and the story of the love match between Richard and the ever loyal Anne Harrison, daughter of Sir John Harrison, of Balls Park, Hertford, is worthy of a book on its own. Thomas was knighted in 1625 after the coronation of Charles I, and he was one of the county's MPs at the start of the war in 1640. Throughout he and his family stuck by the Royalist cause, and suffered because of it.

He was certainly well prepared, for when the Earl of Bedford with his troop of horse visited Ware Park on 29 August 1642, they found 'two pieces of ordinance, with several barrels of powder, muskets, and pike.' It was known he had more, and a report went on 'it is thought he is a great deal better provided, having kept two gunsmiths these three months in his house to mend and make arms clean, but for the present we cannot learn where they are bestowed.' Sir Thomas was away with the king at the time, probably at Nottingham, where the king was about to raise his standard.

He was taken prisoner at the Battle of Worcester, and he and his son were imprisoned and had their estates sequestrated. But at the restoration he was again made MP for the county and in 1661 was created Viscount Fanshawe of Drommore.

However, the losses he had sustained proved too much for him, and in 1668 he sold the manor to Sir Thomas Byde, Recorder of London. His son died during his lifetime, and it then went to a grandson, Thomas, and eventually in 1774 to Thomas Hope Byde, who pulled down the original Fanshawe building, and erected what is substantially to be seen at Ware Park today. The house is now the East Herts district office of Hertfordshire Area Health Authority.

Thomas Hope Byde was really the last occupier of the house to act as lord of the manor, and his last act before he died in 1828 was to make a new set of official weights and measures for the town, inscribed with his name. The manor passed from the Byde family in 1846 when it was sold to James Cudden of Norwich. He sold it to Daniel de Castro in 1853, and in 1869 it passed to George Rastrick of Woking.

Like many other towns, Ware's big houses have been taken over by either government or commercial concerns. Probably the finest is Fanham's Hall, now the home of the Building Societies Staff College, but still used for local dinners and social events.

The early history can be traced from 1412 to 1715 when a Queen Anne House was built to replace the original farmhouse. It was enlarged in 1901, and the work must have been costly. Of particular interest are the walnut panelling in the lounge with its inlaid mother-of-pearl, the oak panelling, the minstrels' gallery and the tiled fireplace of the great hall, the oak-panelling and the ceiling of the long gallery, once the picture gallery.

The Queen Anne staircase from the White Hall remains from the original building, and the present oak panelled dining room was the site of the old conservatory. Stained glass plays a part in the decor, including at least one window by pre-Raphaelite William Morris.

The house did not remain in the ownership of any one family until 1859. In 1822 it was bought by Samuel Adams, one of the owners of the Ware Bank. (Many of the malting families were also connected with banking.) The Adams bank was established in 1813, but went bankrupt in 1856. In 1859 the hall was bought by Henry Page, founder of Henry Page and Co. Ltd., the Ware Maltsters, and the house was connnected with the family until December 1950 when it was purchased by Westminster Bank as a staff college.

Henry Page left a large fortune to his daughter Anne, who married Richard Benyon Croft, a member of an ancient Herefordshire family. They brought up two sons and six daughters, and the younger son was created the first Lord Croft. After many years in the House of Commons as Sir Henry Page-Croft, he was made Lord Croft in May 1940, when he joined Churchill's government as Under Secretary of State for War. He died in 1947.

The Japanese Gardens at the hall were designed by a Mr Inaka and laid out by Professor Suzuki. Japanese gardeners came over each summer in pre-war days to carry out work, creating ornamental lakes, and the hill, Little Fuji-yama, and to plant the trees and shrubs. A Japanese tea house is near the Fox-Lake.

With the closing of the manor courts, elections for the Ware Local Board of Health were held in 1849—it says something for the interest in the town that 24 people stood for the nine seats.

The board first sat on 1 September, 1849 with Mr W. Parker as chairman, and Mr. Nathaniel Cobham, clerk. It continued to function until the Public Health Act of 1894, which brought in an urban council consisting of 12 members. In 1973 the urban district was merged into the larger East Herts Council, but the town still has a successor parish council, or town council and the chairman is now known as town mayor.

ABOVE: Part of a charter granted to Robert De Quencey for an annual fair held at Ware. Robert served in the wars in France, and the charter was granted to him by Henry III at Bordeaux in 1254.

BELOW: The old Ware Park Manor, built in about 1590 by Thomas Fanshawe but pulled down and rebuilt in 1774 by Thomas Hope Byde.

Three seals of Ware Priory. ABOVE LEFT: the seal of Prior John (1259-60), RIGHT: possibly another of Prior John's seals, and a similar seal, this time of Prior Ralph (1297).

LEFT: Place House, in Blue Coat yard is believed to be the original Ware Manor House. Later it became the home of the headmaster of Christ's Hospital School, and is to be restored by the Hertfordshire Building Preservation Trust.

RIGHT: A glimpse of the glory of the old manor house—a carved panel now almost past redemption.

ABOVE: The present Ware park, photographed in 1910 before it was badly damaged by fire. It was substantially rebuilt in the same style.

LEFT: Thomas Fanshawe, the Remembrancer of the Exchequer, later knighted, and eventually made Viscount Fanshawe of Dromore.

RIGHT: Thomas Fanshawe's signature.

LEFT: Richard Fanshawe, brother of Thomas, a distinguished diplomat, later Ambassador to the court of Spain in Madrid, where he died in 1666, and RIGHT: Lady Ann Fanshawe, wife of Richard, with one of their 14 children.

LEFT: The memorial to Sir Richard and Lady Fanshawe in St Mary's Church, Ware, and RIGHT: The Fanshawe's are here remembered in Westminster Abbey.

BELOW AND OPPOSITE: The weights and measures given to the town by Thomas Hope Byde in July 1828.

Blue Coat yard, with the row of houses which housed the children of Christ's Hospital School, ABOVE: about 1900, BELOW: Today; Place House is on the right.

Bluecoated Tenants

The original manor house is almost certainly Place House in what is now known as Blue Coat yard. It was Edward VI who set up Christs Hospital School in London in 1552, and it was just after the 1666 fire of London, that children from the school were temporarily dispersed as evacuees, to the homes of 'respectable nurses in the country'. About 62 went to Ware, and 56 to Hertford. Perhaps the fire had nothing to do with it, but although new buildings were erected in London, Place House was bought from William Collett in 1685. The house was partly in ruins and it was ordered to be rebuilt together with cottages for the nurses and children.

Place House—or the old manor—was the master's house, although some of it was probably used for classrooms. Opposite was a row of 12 two-storeyed cottages in which the boys used to live with their nurses. There were probably more cottages, because one undated pamphlet says that the property was 'a fine building like a college, making a large quadrangle and containing a school house and a Master's house and twenty houses for nurses to keep children.' At the far end of the Ware quadrangle Sir Jonathan Raymond provided a field for the boys, who in 1692, numbered 140.

During the headmastership of Mr Hathaway, the field was the source of great controversy, for he kept his own animals, an ass and a cow in it, and 'restrained' the children from playing there 'lest the beasts be frightened or harmed'. Another used it for his geese and fowls.

The boys used to play on the gravel courtyard between the school house and their wards, and scratch marks can still be seen on the boundary walls which remind one of their games of noughts and crosses.

But the school was never really satisfactory. In 1683 the governors on their 'visitation' said the children had made complaints against the master, Mr Haggard. Although the boys were reprimanded for their presumption, the master was also told exactly what his duties were, and promised to perform them.

The children attended St Mary's Church, and as at All Saints, Hertford, a special gallery was erected for them in 1687. This was eventually demolished in 1835.

In 1760 the school was moved to Hertford, but the buildings were retained and leased by the governors until they were sold in 1894.

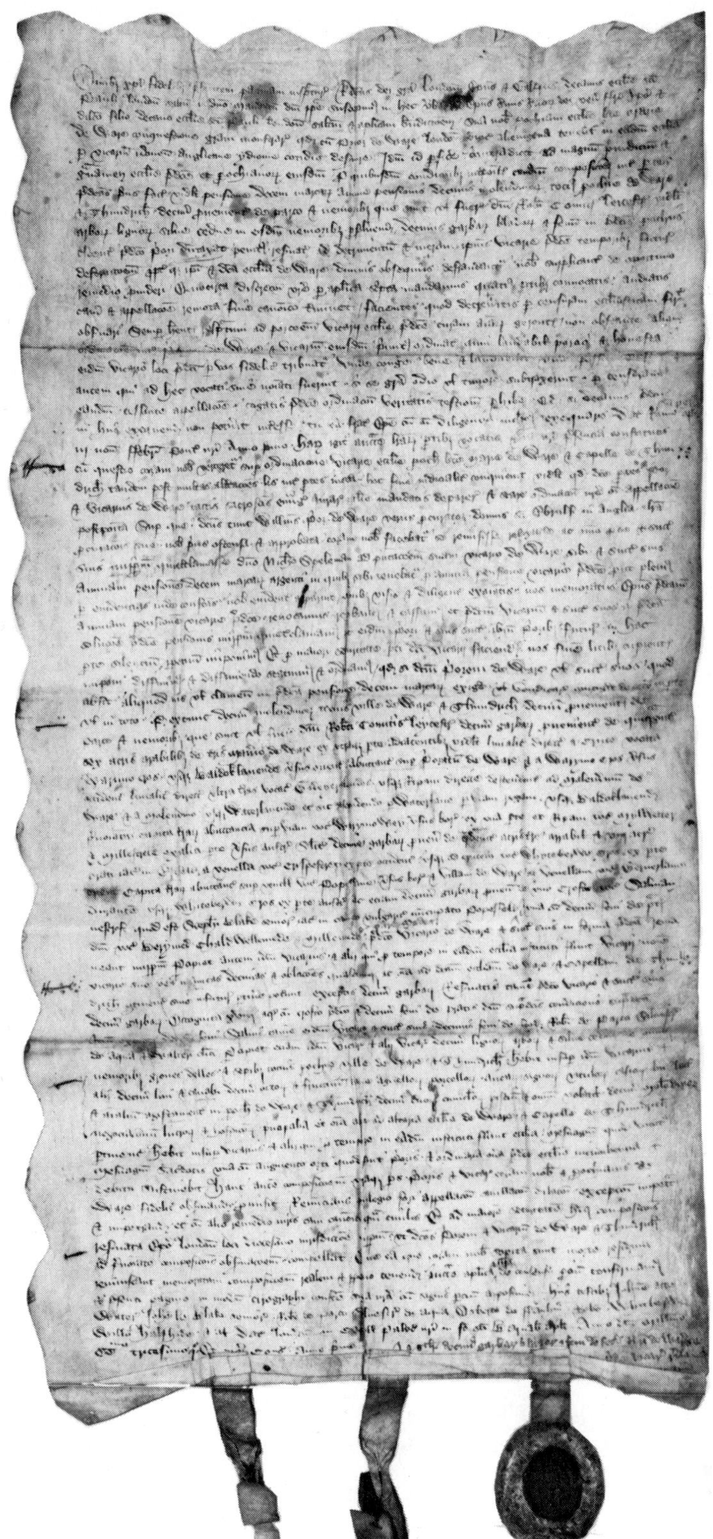

In 1228 the people of Ware complained to Pope Gregory IX that the Prior at Ware would not allow them to have a 'sufficient' vicar. The Pope ordered the Bishop and Dean of London to investigate the complaint and deal with it. This document, known as the Feast of St Barnabas, and dated 1231, was the result. It laid down the rules for the provision of a vicar, and what tithes he was entitled to.

Priors and Friars

The present residence known as The Manor House is more correctly the old Rectory Manor, one of the few remaining pieces of an extensive Alien Benedictine Priory. The building now known as The Priory, was, in fact a Friary.

Hugh de Grentmaisnil, when he became Lord of the Manor, was anxious to present some of his land to the Benedictine Abbey of St Evroul, in Normandy. It was an abbey which he had helped to restore. The Ware land was intended for the foundation of a cell of the abbey. William the Conqueror agreed, and also added the church, already there.

The priory thus established became known as an alien priory, having its main roots outside the country. It was certainly the only one in the county, and probably the most important of the small foundations elsewhere in the country, because the Prior of Ware was the Procter of England of all St Evroul houses.

The priory, naturally, owed financial allegiance to the founding abbey, and this meant sending money out of the country to France. This caused no end of problems, especially when England was engaged in its many and long wars with France. If this gave the priors problems, they also had difficulties with the lords—and ladies—of the Ware Manor.

For instance, in 1219, Margaret de Quencey, on inheriting the manor, made her headquarters at the Priory. She built a great hall, a large chamber, and a chapel for herself, and held her manorial courts there. When her son Roger succeeded her in 1235 he carried on in the same way, as did his brother Robert, who inherited the manor on transfer.

The prior, feeling left out of things, built a small hall for himself, and Joan, daughter of Robert de Quencey, added yet another room for herself. So the priory grew, and although there is no documentation to prove it, it is generally accepted that it stood north of the church, in and around the area now occupied by the Rectory Manor. There was a Priory Farm, which adjoined it, going north, and it was a big and profitable one.

Joan died in 1283, and when the king's men tried to get possession of it, they found it shut up. It was only with the help of the Earl of Gloucester's men that an entry was forced. The prior, meanwhile, had pulled down Joan's new hall.

It was the prior's job to find a priest for the church, but it was not easy—they had to pay him 10 marks a year, and the prior kept all the tithes.

Finally in 1228 the people of Ware rebelled—not for the last time—and they petitioned Pope Gregory IX asking him to see that they had a suitable vicar. The Pope asked the Bishop and Dean of London to look into the matter, and the Prior agreed that he would stand by whatever decision was taken.

The decision is interesting. It gave the vicar a tenth of practically everything, 'except sheaves of corn and of hay, exclusive of the tenths of hay due to the vicar and his successors from the farm of Robert of the Park, Sylvester of the Water, and Walter Clerk.' He was also to have a house, and would be responsible for the expenses of the church. But the Priory then fell in and out of royal hands as the wars with France ebbed and flowed, starting in 1295. A king's overseer was ordered to stay in the Priory to see that there was no contact with France.

This procedure was apparently followed for almost two centuries. Things seemed to be mellowing in 1333, when the Prior made a contribution of 100 shillings towards the expenses of the marriage of Eleanor, the King's sister, to the Count of Gueldres, but it was noted that this would not prejudice the house as a precedent.

The Priory funds were, of course, going to help the royal exchequer, and twice in 1342 and 1343, the prior had difficulty in raising the money due. Yet, in 1342, the prior was granted protection and safe-conduct to attend a general chapter of his order. He went to Normandy with 10 of his men, six horses, and gold for his expenses.

The possessions of all the alien priories had been given for safe custody to the Prior of Monte Acuto in Somerset, and when the peace of Bretigny was signed in 1360, the prior was ordered to restore all the possessions. But war began again in 1367!

Richard II put a hefty burden on the alien priories. He granted to his uncle, Thomas de Wodestok, Earl of Buckingham, £1,000 a year to maintain his rank as earl, the money to come from the farms of the alien priories. Ware was ordered to pay £206 13s 4d.

Prior Herbert, who had been granted custody of the Priory, lost it in 1385. Custody of the manor was given to John Golofre, one of the gentlemen of the king's chamber.

Another blow came in 1395 when the king favoured another of his uncles, Thomas, Duke of Gloucester, with £1,000 a year from alien priories—and again Ware had to pay £206 13s 4d. But the end was in sight for the alien priories. Soon after Henry V came to the throne, in 1413, the alien priories were suppressed, and the Ware priory and all its possessions were granted to the king's new foundation, the Carthusian Priory, the House of Lord Jesus of Bethlehem, at Sheen. This, to all intents and purposes, put an end to the priory's religious life, although the Carthusians continued to keep on the farm because it was a money-spinner.

Efforts were made by the Abbey of St. Evroul to get the property back, and an appeal was made to the Carthusians of Sheen in 1416 but after 11 years, and further appeal to the Pope, they finally gave up the quest.

The knock-out blow came in 1546, when Henry VIII presented the priory and all its property to Trinity College, Cambridge, which still owns small pieces of land in Ware, and still appoints the vicar of St Mary's Church.

It was not until 1951, however, that the college sold the old manor house, the garden, the adjoining steward's house, which had been turned into two cottages, and another adjacent cottage. They were purchased by Sir Stephen Chapman. He made the purchases on the death of his father, who had been the tenant since 1924.

Experts believe that it is certainly a survival of the mediaeval priory, having a timber frame and flint foundations, and it was probably the dormitory wing. The priory farm was in production until the last century.

Until 1848, what is now called the Manor House was known as the Old Rectory, and when the priory farm buildings were finally demolished in 1849, a school was built on the site. Some of the stone-work was also used to face two cottages in Musley Hill.

But what about the building now known as Ware Priory? Strictly speaking it should be Ware Friary. The Franciscan Grey friars were granted a licence by Edward III in 1338, to 'erect an oratory house and other buildings then necessary.' This grant was confirmed in September 1350 by the Pope.

It was one of three sites north of the Alps which the Order had agreed to—three other sites were in Italy. The establishment of the Friary came through the generosity of Thomas, second Lord Wake of Liddell, who was then Lord of the Manor. On his death, his widow, Blanche, was given permission to grant the Friary more land.

For about 200 years it seems to have had a quieter existence than the Priory. There are notes of a number of legacies left to the Friary, including one from Elizabeth de Burgh, Lady Clare (founder of Clare College, Cambridge), who in 1355 left the Friary 40 shillings.

There is a record that in 1430 Roger Downe, a doctor of Oxford, and 35th Minister Provincial of the Order in England, went there for his last years, and when, during 1455, after the Battle of St Albans, Henry VI and his family stayed at Hertford Castle, the Duke of York stayed at the Friary.

Trouble visited Paul, Warden of the Friary in about 1525. He upset the Bishop of London, when he was alleged to have said: 'It is a pity that there be so many images suffered in so many places, where indiscreet and unlearned people be, for they make their prayers and oblations so entirely and heartily before the image that they believe it to be the very saint in heaven.

'Item, that if he knew his father and mother were in heaven, he would count them as good as St Peter and Paul, but for the pain they suffered for Christ's sake.'

He was also supposed to have said that there was no need to go on a pilgrimage, and, the ultimate: 'Item, that if a man were on the point of drowning or in other danger, he should call only upon God and no saint, for saints in heaven cannot help us, neither know they more what men do in this world, than a man in the north country knoweth what is done in the south country.' Paul had to make a swift retraction.

There was some disagreement, earlier in 1395, when the Ware Friars got into trouble with their brothers at Cambridge. Their chief occupation was begging, and the Cambridge affair was a question of demarcation.

The Cambridge men, after pointing out that because the university was in their town they had a tremendous number of visitors to feed, complained that the Ware men seemed to be stretching their begging bowls so far towards Cambridge that the house there was suffering. The Ware men were stopped from extending their boundaries any further than within five miles of the old Cambridge area—except as far as Puckeridge, which Cambridge wanted to keep.

Thomas Chapman was probably the last leader of the Ware Grey Friars. On 5 May 1534, he made a declaration of obedience to Henry VIII and Queen Anne, and agreed to the legality of their marriage. At the same time he repudiated the Pope's authority, and acknowledged the king as supreme head of the church.

A year later the Friary surrendered, although it took a long time for the winding up. Even in 1539 the king's commissioners were still touring the religious houses, and they made detailed expense accounts of their visits. For Ware their expenses included supper, wine and sugar, the minstrels, and fires in their rooms.

First secular tenant of the Friary was Robert Byrche, who paid a rent of 29s 8d a year. He was described as a yeoman of the crown. In 1685 the Friary became the property of Robert Hadsley of Great Munden, and it remained in the Hadsley family until 1868. Clement Morgan then bought it, and sold it to Mr T. Gwyn Jeffreys, who studied sea shells. He lived there until 1881, when the Friary was sold to Mr. Robert Walters, the last private inhabitant. Finally it was purchased by Mrs R. B. Croft, who presented it to the town. It then became the offices of Ware Urban Council, and now the Ware Town Council has offices there, together with the housing department of East Herts District Council.

One of the few treasures of the house, a 14th century refectory table, was recognised as such in 1934, and has been cleaned and treated as a treasure. It is probably older than any part of the building, and was part of the original furniture.

Yet the old religious connections are still in Ware. Poles, formerly the home of a branch of the Hanbury family, is now a convent school, and in the Ware Park area there is a Carmelite Monastery, housing an enclosed order for women.

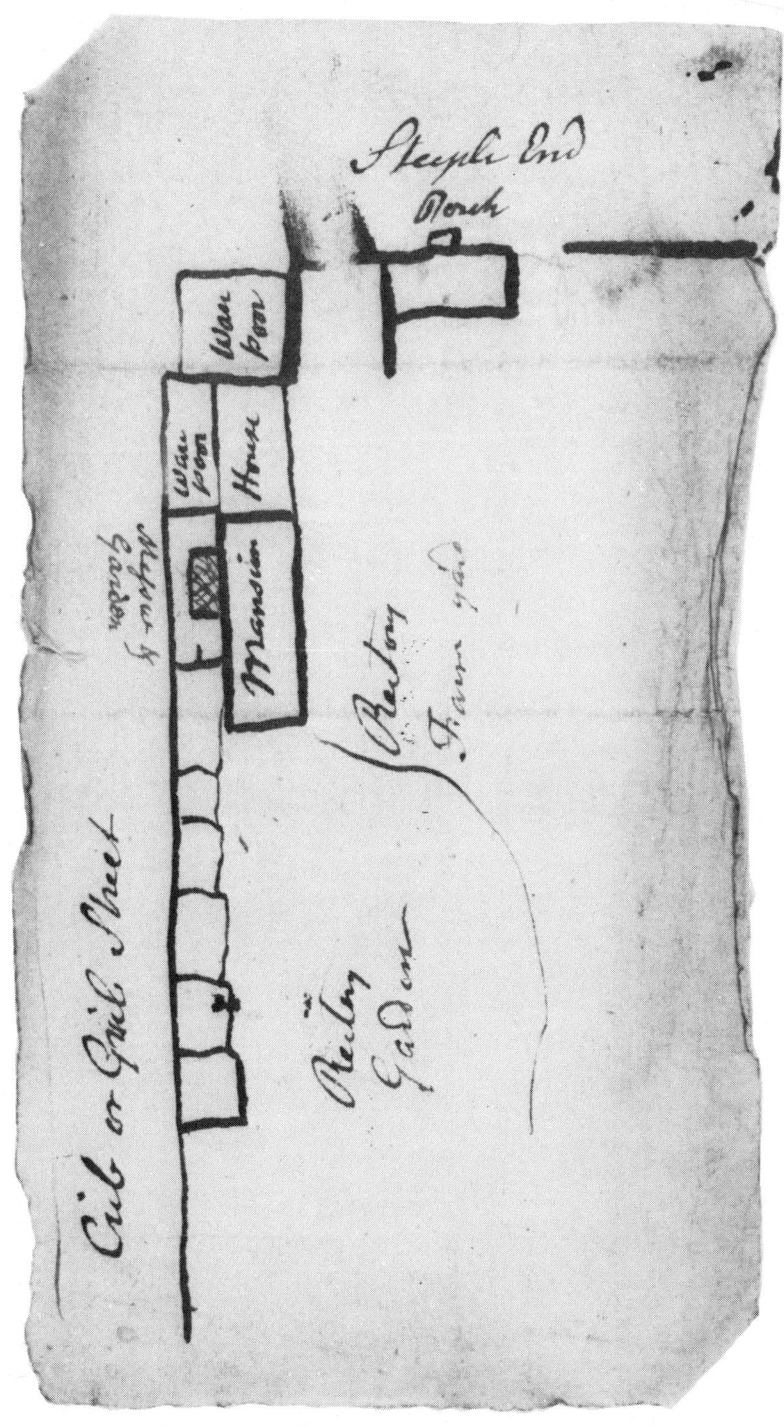

A sketch dated 1778 of the Rectory Manor glebe lands, showing the Mansion House—now known as The Manor, and Crib Street. It is interesting to note that the street opposite to the entrance to the Mansion House is called Steeple End.

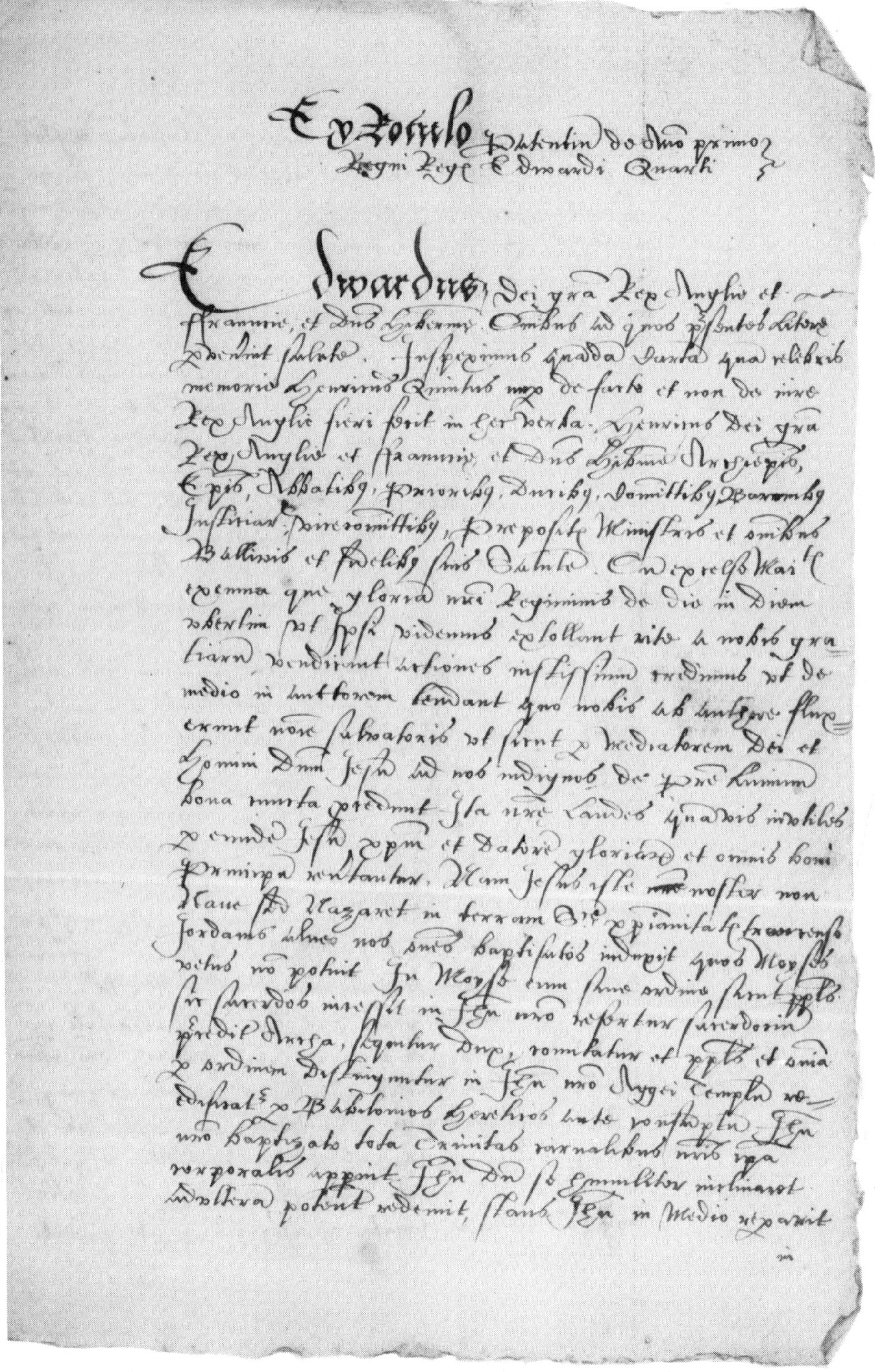

In 1414 the Alien Benedictine Priory was suppressed by Henry V, and granted to the Carthusian Priory at Sheen. In 1461 Edward IV confirmed the gift. This is the first page of a seven page document confirming this and other gifts.

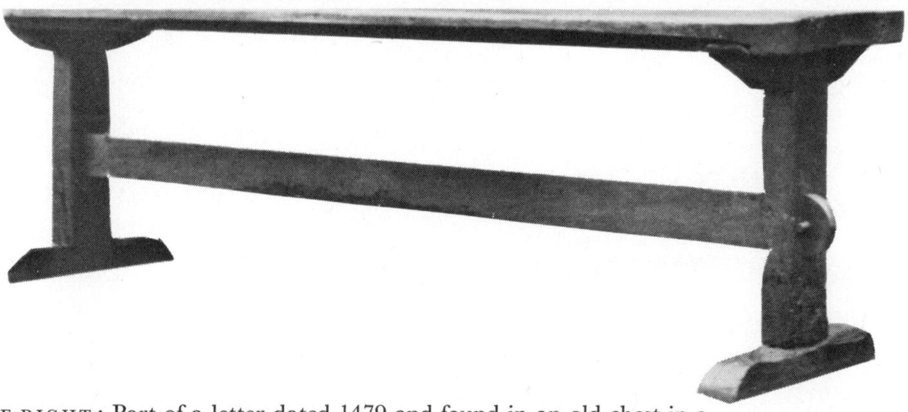

ABOVE RIGHT: Part of a letter dated 1479 and found in an old chest in a cottage at Cherry's Green, Westmill, Buntingford; from Brother John of Ware Friary to John and Alice Aleby, welcoming them into the fraternity.

CENTRE LEFT: A drawing by Dr G. R. Owst of the seal of Ware Friary, found on a document dated 1526.

CENTRE RIGHT: Ware Friary as it looked in about 1820. The drawing is by Thomas Fisher (1771-1836).

BELOW: The 14th century refectory table still housed at the Friary (now known as the Priory).

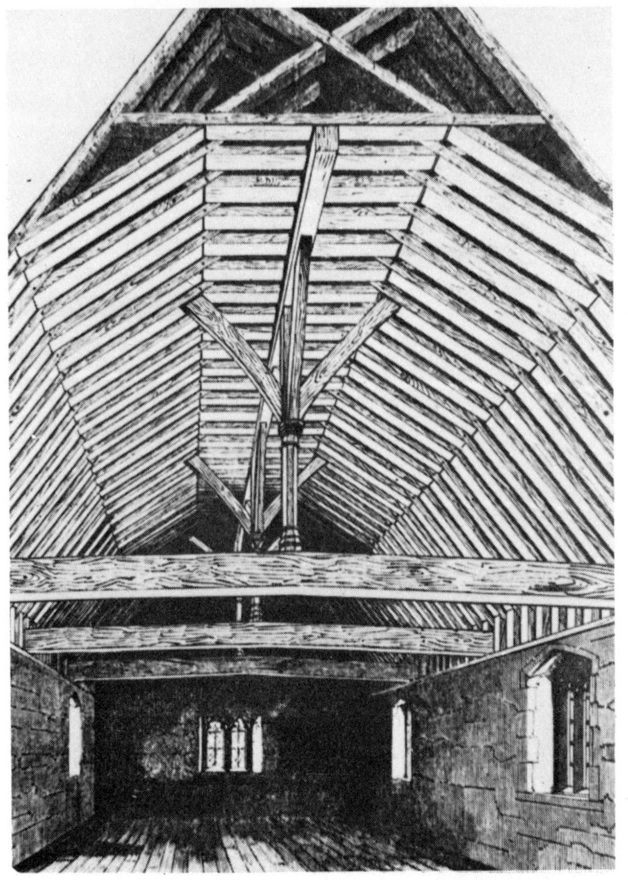

ABOVE: The back of the Friary (Priory) facing onto the river, 1811.

RIGHT: An original king post.

LEFT: The Guest House before alterations; a drawing from The Builder, 1849.

ABOVE: The Friary (Priory) as a private house. This picture of the morning room was taken in 1868.

BELOW: The Suite Gallery in 1865.

ABOVE: A modern view of the front of the Friary (Priory), and
BELOW: The river frontage.

ABOVE: A view of the council chamber in the Priory. Through the door on the left can be seen the Mayor's parlour, with pictures of former civic leaders.

LEFT: Mrs Anne Elizabeth Croft, of Fanhams Hall, who gave the Priory to the town on February 12th, 1920.

RIGHT: The house in Ware Park which is now a Carmelite Monastery.

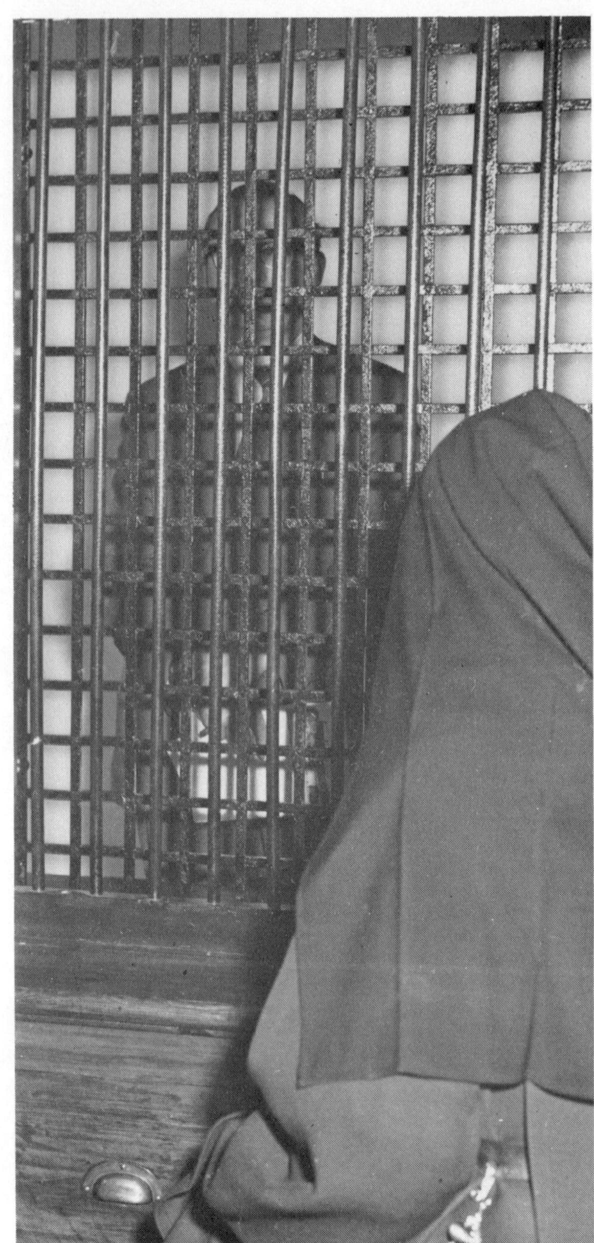

LEFT: A Sister sits in her cell in the Carmelite Monastery, an enclosed order for women.

RIGHT: A visitor speaks to a sister through the grille at the Carmelite Monastery.

Ware-Farers

It is communication by road and river that has made Ware what it is today: a hard-working, industrious town, known far more widely than its size would suggest. Road and river have brought people and goods to and through Ware, and also taken them away again, but not without some difficulty.

With the Roman crossing which took Ermine Street over the Lee in ruins, and no Saxon bridge builders, trade and people must have deserted any settlement there might have been. Traffic still used a great deal of Ermine Street, but diverted to Hertford to cross the ford, and then rejoined the Roman highway.

However, we do know that Ware had a river crossing before the Conquest, and King Harold, in his exhausting march from the battle of Stamford to Hastings, used what was known as the old North Road through the town. We also know that there was a settlement there, because 20 years later Domesday Book provides documentary proof.

In the Hundred Rolls of Edward I it is established that the bridge was part of the king's highway, and that Henry III had recognised this. The roll also records '. . . the bailiff and men of Ware have turned aside the way that used to pass by Hertford to Ware to the detriment of the town of Hertford'.

Records then begin to show a number of distinguished visitors using the road. The town played a small part in the starting of the Wars of the Roses. In 1455, Richard, Duke of York arrived in Ware with his troops, and sent a messenger to London, asking Henry VI that a conference might be arranged.

The king's advisers kept the message from him, and he left for St. Albans. Receiving no reply, the Duke of York took this as a challenge, and hastened to St Albans. So began the long and bitter conflict between the white and red rose.

Tolls were paid on items passing over the bridge—hence the anger of Hertford bailiffs when they lost control of the bridge. For instance, in 1485 there was a toll of twopence 'for every cart carrying woollen cloth, hides, wine and other merchandise and other things for sale passing over the bridges of Ware and Hertford or elsewhere: for every pack-horse laden with things for sale of which the pack is bound with cord or other fastenings under the horse's stomach one penny, but if there be no fastening, then one half penny, except the horse be carrying corn for itself, then one farthing;

for every man going over the bridge and elsewhere and carrying on his back merchandise and other things for sale the value of which exceeds four sterling, one shilling.'

The town seemed to be a convenient distance from London for rest on a journey, and for those going to the capital an over-night stop so that the traveller could arrive refreshed in the morning.

Thomas Cromwell lodged in the town, when, as Henry VIII's minister, he was on his way to Yorkshire to quell a rebellion. He moved on from there to Huntingdon. During this period the town regularly cropped up in royal letters as ministers of state, heralds, and dignitaries stayed the night.

James I used the road and passed through Ware on many occasions, the first of which was when he came down from Scotland to be crowned.

The funeral procession of Mary, Queen of Scots, passed through Ware on 7 October 1612, on its way from Peterborough to Westminster. James again in 1617 went north, setting out from Theobalds, at Waltham Cross. His queen, Anne of Denmark, travelled with him to Ware and then returned. She died in 1619. In that year Sir Lewis Watson wrote to his cousin Sir Edward Montague: 'The king is pretty well recovered, and came last night to Ware, so to Tiballes (Theobalds) during pleasure. The gout is gotten into one of his knees which makes him to be carried all the way in a chair.'

The condition of the road was causing problems, and it must have been bad—almost a national joke. In December 1641 Lord Digby, in the House of Lords, made an attack on the Commons, and a writer to Sir Edward Montague described it thus: 'He bespattered them as much as one would do his cloak in riding from Ware to London.'

High Street saw something of an argument which must have been talked about for a long time in May 1639. Lord Ker, the Earl of Roxburgh's son, was on his way north with letters from the Queen. The Postmaster, whose duty it was to find him fresh horses, for some strange reason decided to take a large cart horse which had taken corn to market. The owner would not part with it, quite correctly saying that his horse was not fit to be a post horse. The Postmaster and the poor countryman shouted at each other in the street, and were heard by three Deputy-Lieutenants and JPs, Sir Richard Lucy, Sir John Butler, and Sir John Watts. They ruled that the cart-horse was not fit for the post, and told the Postmaster to find animals more fit for the service.

This hit the Postmaster's dignity, and he went back to complain to Lord Ker. Now his lordship became annoyed. He found out where the deputy-lieutenants' horses were kept and commanded that three of them should be used to carry the post. But the three knights would not hear of it, and the hot-tempered Lord Ker challenged the three justices to a fight in a nearby field.

Sir John Butler and Sir John Watts were prepared to go, but Sir Richard, knowing that Lord Ker had a case of pistols by his side, decided that he would try authority instead of arms. He sent out for post-horses, and then told Lord Ker that there were horses available for him. If he did not take them he would be bound, the letters taken from him, and delivered by other means. Lord Ker cooled down a little, and, still grumbling, agreed to take the horses provided. But the justices wrote to Lord Salisbury, who was then the county's Lord Lieutenant, telling the whole incident, and arranged for their complaint to be at court as soon as Lord Ker.

It was King James himself who called on the justices sitting at Buntingford and Ware, to stop all wheeled traffic during the winter between Royston, Buntingford and Ware, to give the road a rest. The result of this ban should have been that all malting traffic—the town's life blood—was carried on packhorses. But the rule was sometimes relaxed, and the occasional cart with two wheels and drawn by only five horses, was allowed through.

Then in 1663 the justices of Hertford, Cambridge, and Huntingdon complained to parliament that: 'the ancient highway and postroad leading from London to York and so into Scotland . . . by reason of the great and many loads which are weekly drawn in waggons to Ware (whence there was water-carriage to London) and the great trade in barley and malt, is become so ruinous and almost impassable that the ordinary course appointed by all former laws and statutes of this realm is not sufficient for the effectual repairing of the same.'

Parliament, in its wisdom, decided to put up three toll-gates, the revenue from which would go to repair the road. One was to be at Caxton in Cambridgeshire, one in Stilton in Huntingdonshire, and the other at Wadesmill, just up the road from Ware.

At Stilton there was so much local opposition that the toll-gate was never erected; at Caxton it was so easily evaded as to be useless, so the Wadesmill toll-gate became the first of its kind in England.

That it was necessary is proved in the documents of Herts County Sessions in 1646-7 where it says: 'The great decay of all the ways arises through the unreasonable loads of malt brought into and through Ware to Hodsdon from remote parts, and the bringing of great loads of malt from both the Hadhams, Alburie, Starford, all the Pelhams and Clavering, through Ware Extra (Wareside) and the excessive loads from Norwich, Bury, and Cambridge weekly, the teams often consisting of seven or eight horses. There is a great increase of maltsters in Ware.'

Samuel Pepys told in his diary of the bad roads, recording: '17 September, 1661 we got to Ware (he was with his wife), and there supped, and to bed very merry and pleasant. The next morning up early and begun our march; the way about Puckridge very bad, and my wife, in the very last dirty place of all, got a fall, but no hurt, though some dirt. At last she begun, poor wretch, to be tired, and I to be angry at it, but I was to blame; for she is a very good companion as long as she is well.'

Again on 15 October 1662, 'Will (his servant) and I came to Ware about three o'clock in the afternoon, the ways being everywhere very bad.'

The toll had an adverse effect on trade in Ware. It appears that carts bringing goods into the town had to pay a fee, and if they returned empty the same day they went back through for nothing. If they stayed overnight in Ware, they had to pay to go back through the toll gate.

Ware traders, especially the innkeepers, petitioned the Sessions court, saying that carters and drovers were going back to the other side of the toll the same day to get a night's lodgings instead of staying in Ware as they had done previously. The court saw the point, and ruled that if a waggon returned empty within 12 hours that would count as the same day, and the dues would not have to be paid.

Tolls there may have been, but the road appears to have improved little. A Fellow of the Royal Society, Ralph Thoresby, recorded in 1695: 'Rode by Puckeridge to Ware, where we baited, and had some showers, which raised the washes upon the road to that height that passengers from London that were upon the road, swam, and a poor higgler was drowned, which prevented our travelling for many hours, yet towards evening adventured with some country people.'

Things had certainly improved by 1724, when Daniel Defoe, in his tour around Great Britain wrote: 'Though this road is continually work'd upon, by the vast numbers of Carriages, bringing Malt and Barley to Ware, for whose sake indeed, it was obtained; yet, with small repairs it is maintain'd and the Toll is reduced from a penny to a halfpenny.'

Tales of highwaymen abound on the road, and even in 1784, when the young Italian, Vincent Lunardi, made the first balloon flight over English soil, landing near High Cross, he was escorted to Bayfordbury, home of Sir William Baker, along by-roads, via the Bull at Ware, for fear of highwaymen.

Because the road formed part of Ware High Street, there were frequent complaints about lack of repairs, but now, with the new by-pass flying over the meads, High Street is quieter—at least that is the theory of road-builders and planners. But the old North Road, although the most important, was not the only one at Ware, and Norden's map of 1598 shows that all the five roads centered on the town were of equal size.

They were also in the same state of disrepair. The road to Hertford was always in trouble, and particularly after the construction of the New River. It was claimed in 1646 that the banks of the river needed repairing, and because of this damage was being caused to the highway. Several times Sir William Myddelton, son of the river's originator, was asked to make the repairs, but to no avail.

It eventually got to the stage where men were falling into the river and drowning, and waggons, carts, and horses went into the stream.

In 1768 matters came to a head, as a letter to the inhabitants of Hertford, dated 1771, puts it: 'In 1768 a road in Herts which had for time immemorial been suffered to remain impassable by all carriages (narrow-wheeled carts and waggons excepted) became the subject of universal complaint but nothing was done. At length . . . a person who frequently suffered inconvenience from the road, availing himself of the powers granted, as Surveyor of Amwell, by the late General Highway Act (1766) and assisted in the execution thereof by some gentlemen in the Commission of the Peace . . . applied the whole statute duty of the parish, with the addition of parochial rates and liberal subscriptions of his own, to improving that part of the road . . . which, by these means and the generous aid of a gentleman in Ware, was completed to the satisfaction of the public.'

Now, who was that 'generous gentleman'? Tradition suggests it was John Scott, the Quaker poet, who lived alongside the road, in Amwell House, now part of Ware College. Lawrence D. Stewart, who has written a fine book on Scott, says: 'In view of the three tragedies which came into his own life in 1768, it seems incredible that Scott should, in the same year, have found time or inclination to supervise the building of the main thoroughfare between Ware and Hertford.'

He does not, however, discount the possibility. There is ample evidence that he was interested in highways, and in 1778 he was trustee of the Cheshunt, Wadesmill, and Watton turnpikes. He wrote several books on highways, and on highway law, and is credited with improving the principal streets of Ware.

The Ware Extra, or Upland road to Wareside and beyond, was also an important highway. It was used in 1447 for the funeral procession of the Duke of Gloucester, which rested at Ware on its way to St Albans. The tradition of 'ruinous' roads persisted here too. In 1598 there was a presentment which said: 'The highway between Ware and Widford is very ruinous and the inhabitants of Ware ought to repair the same.'

The road to Watton-at-Stone, now the B1001, was built by Sayer de Quencey, Earl of Winchester, and the Lord of the Manor at Ware, during the reign of King John. The road had an unfortunate effect on Hertford. Before it was built, traffic from the north-west going to Ware had to pass through the county town. The new road by-passed Hertford, and all that implied.

The road was used by the Magna Carta barons when they were invited to London in 1215—and de Quencey was one of them. King John, it appeared, hated Sayer 'worse than viper's blood'.

This road, too, receives official condemnation. A presentment in 1620 says that Ware parish should repair it, but by 1772 it had become a turnpike. An order by the Trustees said: 'Any number of horses, not exceeding ten, may be used for drawing up waggons and carriages with 9in wheels; and not exceeding six for waggons of less breadth for the purpose of drawing up three hills in that part of the road between Watton and Ware, from and to such parts of them as are hereafter mentioned. . . .'

The roads still exist, and apart from the new by-pass, follow almost the way they did four centuries ago. They have played their part, and a major one, in the history of the town, but perhaps not such a big one as the river.

LEFT: The Tudor gateway of the Black Swan, which was in Baldock Street.

RIGHT: James I passed through Ware and stayed at inns in the town 'with his hawks'.

BELOW: A 14th century Ware window frame, now in Hertford Museum.

ABOVE: Ware market square, 1817.

BELOW: Houses in Baldock Street, 1838.

ABOVE: The Bulls Head, Baldock Street, pictured in 1925. An inn with that name is mentioned in documents as early as 1572.

CENTRE: No 63 High Street is one of the finest old Ware houses. The main room on the first floor has a barrelled ceiling, and this design above the overmantel. On it are the letters H.I.S. and the date 1624.

BELOW: The gateway into the yard of 63 High Street, formerly the Royal Oake, first documented in 1664.

ABOVE: Rankin Square in about 1910. The town hall, centre, was one of two in the town, run by the Old Town Hall Syndicate which started in about 1870, and was still alive in 1940.

BELOW: The second town hall.

LEFT: The Old Punch House in Rankin Square, certainly well-known in early Victorian days as a resort for the elderly gentlemen. There was a spacious coffee room at the rear, divided into boxes.

RIGHT: Kibes Lane, in the early 1920s before it became a car park, with all the old houses demolished.

BELOW: Bridgefoot, Ware, about 1900. On the left is the narrow Star Street.

ABOVE: Baldock Street in 1911.

CENTRE: The milkman delivers his wares in Musley Hill, in 1919.

BELOW: The new Ware by-pass (A10), here opened in August 1976.

ABOVE: A print of Ware river from the Gerish collection.

BELOW: Sailing barges at Ware, about 1830.

Waterway

The River Lee, Lea, Ley, or Luy are all names given to the stream which has not only beautified the town, but has contributed to its prosperity in times past. It was after the defeat of the Danes in the ninth century that Ware was established as a Saxon village, and this coincided with the use of the Lee as a waterway. Edward the Elder founded the settlement two years after setting up the twin burghs at Hertford, about 913-14. Two water mills were set up, one beside the Roman crossing. Here there was a natural fall in the river and the lock was built later (1767). The river also went into two channels, one of which became the mill stream. The old mill site is now occupied by Allen and Hanburys Ltd. The second mill was east of the bridge, and Spillers French Milling Ltd. have premises there.

As we know, the Lee figured in quarrels between Hertford and Ware, and the Bailiffs of Hertford were always complaining about the Lords of the Ware manor. The Hundred rolls tell it all: 'The Lady of Ware and her bailiffs have neglected the weirs of Ware so that no boats can pass as accustomed', or 'The lady and bailiffs of Ware have altered the weirs of Ware to the great annoyance of the burgesses of Hertford, and to the detriment of the town of Hertford.'

Peace broke out in 1207, when the Countess of Leicester and the Hertford bailiff agreed that tolls from all ships laded at Ware were to be divided between them, reserving free carriage to the Countess for her wares, and free passage for the boats from Hertford. Yet neglect of the river led to a great flood in the early 15th century, which almost destroyed the town.

Barges were certainly in use on the Lee in 1423, and several petitions were raised in Henry VI's reign to try to improve the condition of the river. In 1440 Sir Ralph Cromwel, Knt, John Fray, Robert Rolleston and others agreed to remove all the shelves and shoals in the river. It was referred to as 'One of the great rivers which extends from the Town of Ware to the water of the Thames.' However by Tudor times, corn and malt leaving Ware for London were carried by road to Enfield before being loaded into barges.

An Act of Parliament of 1571 saw the Lee Navigation become a reality, and £80,000 was spent on improving the river, and the erection of locks. This was the first river improvement in England. But this infuriated the Enfield bargemen, who damaged the new locks and tried to sink Ware barges with gunpowder.

How did the barges work? They loaded at Ware on a Saturday, and on Monday went to Bow Bridge where they waited for the tide. From there it took them four hours to get to London's centre. It took them six hours to get from Ware to Waltham Cross, and another six hours to Bow.

It was during the Great Plague that Ware bargemen carved themselves a place in history. They continued carrying corn to London, and helped greatly in saving the city from starvation. For this service, Charles II granted privileges to Ware to be 'enjoyed for all time.'

Ware barges have been entitled to enter the Thames without taking the service of a lighterman, and the bargees on their return home from a trip could demand refreshment at any hour. Strangely enough, although these privileges have been exercised since 1665, and are recognised by the Port of London Authority, nothing has ever been traced in writing.

The bargemen did their bit again in 1667 with the Dutch at the mouth of the Thames. Coal, which was mined in the Midlands, and shipped down the East coast from King's Lynn, went by water to Cambridge, by land to Ware, and then by river to London.

Another milestone in the history of the river came in 1609 when a start was made on the New River, as an additional supply of water for London. The original start was near Emma's Well, from which Great Amwell gets its name. By tradition Emma was the wife of Canute, who it is said lived there, and enjoyed the water from the well, which is just below the church.

Sir Hugh Myddelton, an alderman and goldsmith of the City of London, MP for Denbigh, with mining interests in Cardiganshire, offered to build the river, and took four years to cut from Amwell to Clerkenwell. When only a quarter of the work was completed, Sir Hugh's money ran out, and the Corporation refused to help, but James I provided the balance. He covered himself, however, by accepting shares in the company. Under George II additional water was allowed to be drawn from the Lee, and the gauge house stands on the riverside between Hertford and Ware. In 1904 the undertaking was transferred to the Metropolitan Water Board, and is now under the wing of the Thames Water Authority. In the 19th century the New River Company shares fetched astronomical prices. But the Lee, like Ware's roads, was constantly the subject of complaints as to its condition, and its dangers.

When Ware lock was rebuilt in 1831, something of the past of the town was rediscovered. Skeletons, a portion of 'steel-yard'—probably Roman—a brass coin of Domitian, a brass candlestick, an iron axe head, a finger ring, a hairpin, a Roman key, and a brass coin of Severus were all recovered.

During the 1914-18 war the river filled an exciting role, for special boats to carry ammunition to France were built and launched in Ware docks. In more peaceful times the river, with its many riverside summerhouses or gazebos, has enhanced the beauty of the town. May they return.

ABOVE: The river in 1920 showing the summer houses (Gazebos) in good condition. In the distance is the old iron bridge which spanned the river.

BELOW: A well-dressed lady takes a walk on the iced-over river in January 1891.

ABOVE: Barge traffic was still considerable in 1930; CENTRE: The river in 1893.

BELOW: Isaac Walton loved the River Lee and the modern fisherman, with all his tackle, is no exception.

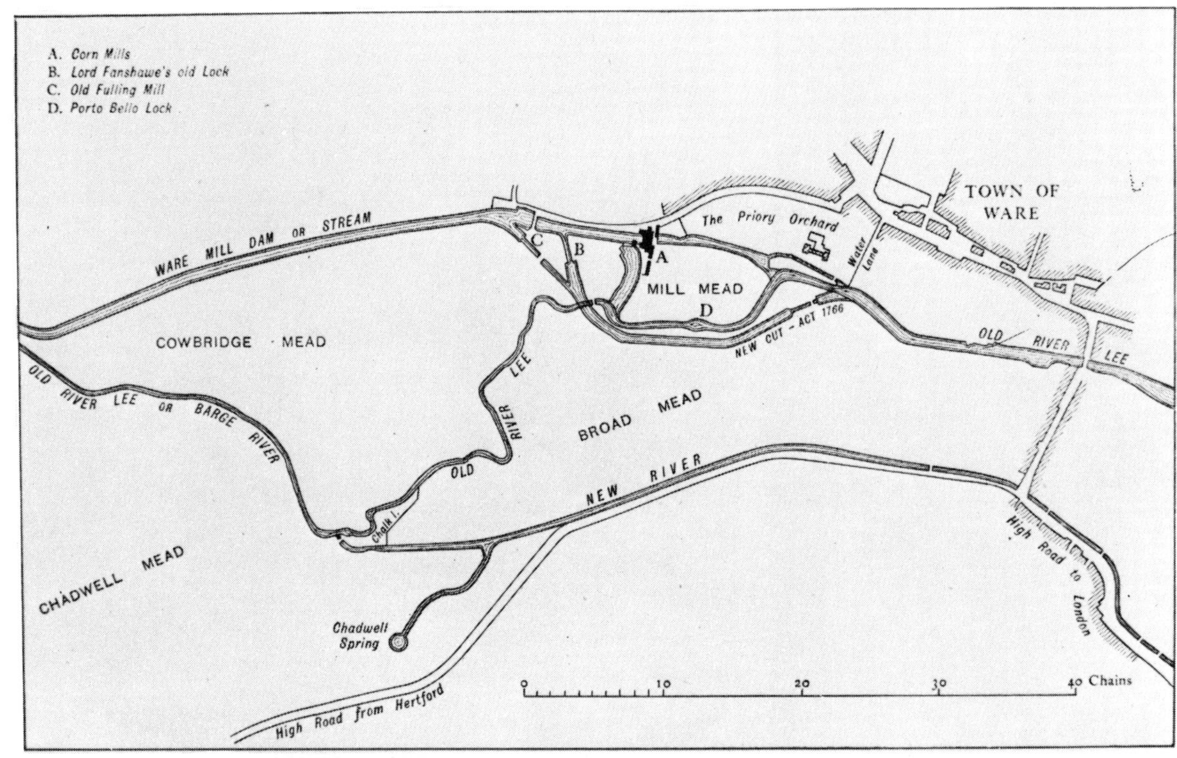

ABOVE: A plan of the River Lee showing the 1831 alterations.

BELOW: The river in 1905.

The modern river and the derelict gazebos.

ABOVE: New River head—the start of the New River, which in the 17th century, was designed to take drinking water to London.

BELOW: Sir Hugh Myddelton, who in 1609 started the New River, originally from Great Amwell. It was later extended to Ware.

A drawing by Eleanor Tyler

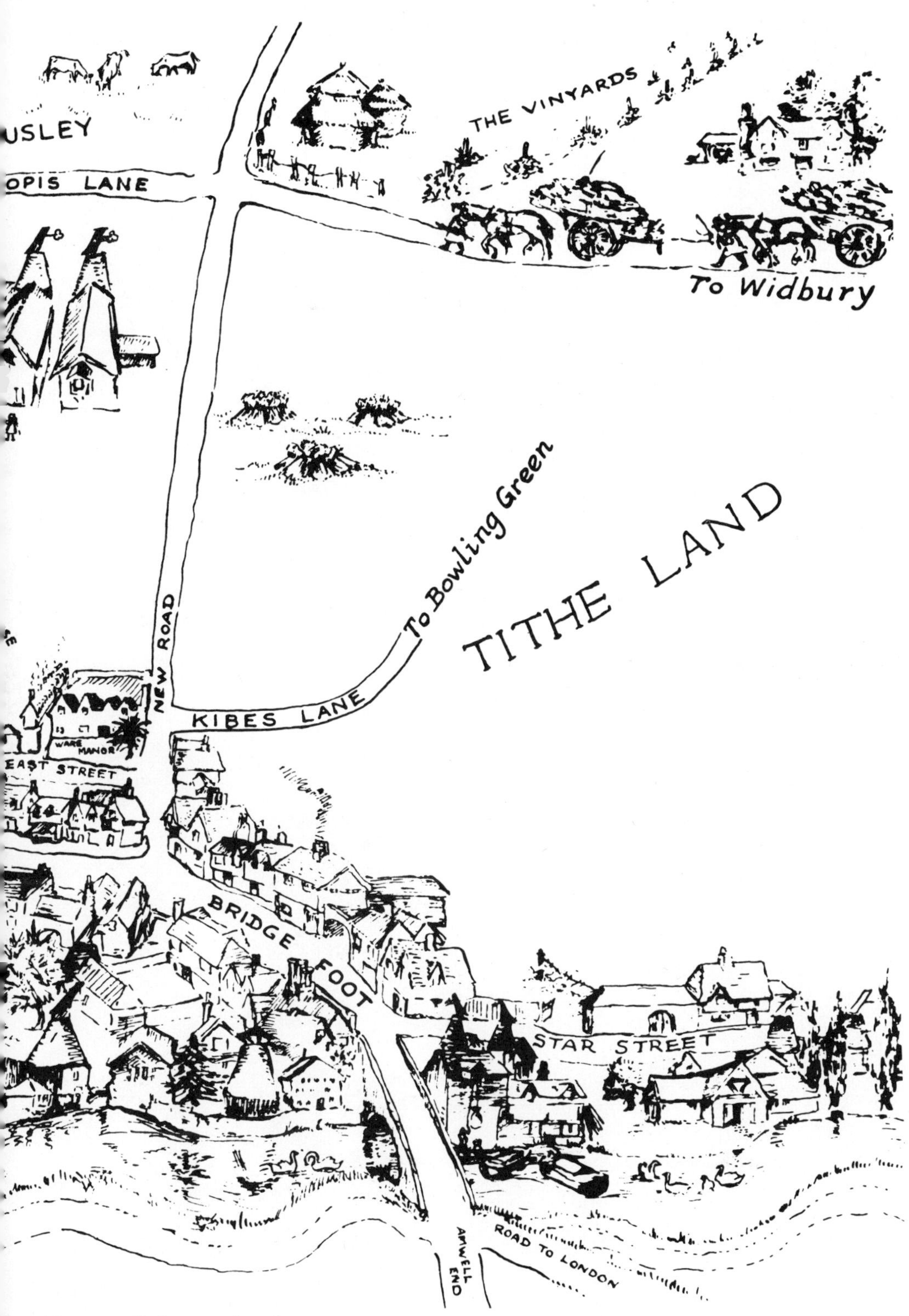

the old town relied on road and

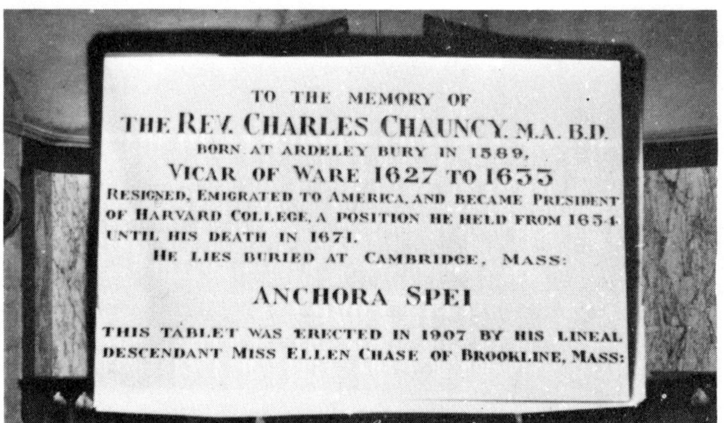

LEFT: One of the many tabards which adorned St Mary's Church before the church was restored—a drawing in the Oldfield collection *c*1800—probably that of the Fanshawe family.

RIGHT: Charles Chauncy, Vicar of Ware from 1627 to 1633, and later President of Harvard University in America, and BELOW: A tablet to the Rev Charles Chauncy erected in St Mary's Church by a descendant, Miss Ellen Chase, of Brookline, Mass. in 1907.

Plain Preachers

Ware had a church in 1078. It was mentioned in the charter given by William I to Hugh de Grentmaisnil, and between that date and 1415 there are various accounts of the problems of providing a parish priest, but there is nothing in writing about the building as such, or where it was. It seems logical to assume it was close by the Alien Benedictine Priory, which was probably clustered around the present site of the church of St Mary the Virgin.

The present church dates to what is known as the decorated period, 1245 to 1360. Parts of the chancel are 13th century, but the rest, together with the west tower, is Perpendicular—1360 to 1485. Most of the roof is 15th century, but that of the chancel is modern.

Like so many English churches, it has suffered from reformers and restorers, and most of the brasses and monuments it once contained have been swept away. Experts and tradition disagree over one of its prized possessions, the font. The experts date it to about 1380, but tradition says it was the gift of Thomas Montagu, Earl of Salisbury, husband of Alianore, who inherited Ware Manor in 1408.

The font is octagonal, and on each of the panels is carved a figure under a moulded arch. These represent St Margaret, St Christopher, St George, St Katherine, St James, St John the Baptist, and two panels contain representations of the Annunciation.

The 1847-9 restoration, though necessary according to accounts in the *Hertfordshire Mercury* of the time, nevertheless swept away the last vestige of a church which had seen much pomp and circumstance. Tombs and brasses went; so too did a rather large remnant of wall paintings.

The *Mercury* account described an ugly lumbering gallery in the north transept, blocking 'a large and elegant "imbricated" window'. It was built for the Christs Hospital boys in 1687. The west end of the church also had a gallery which contained the organ.

Whether all the brasses went with reform is open to doubt because they started to disappear soon after 1800, and Cooke's *Pocket County Directory* attributes this to pillage by a 'knavish Sexton'. We also know from James Smith of Melbourne, writing in the *Mercury* that in about 1840 the church was hung with tattered banners and rusty helmets.

The living of the church remained with the priory until 1415, when Henry V passed it to his Carthusian Priory at Sheen. Henry VIII granted the church and the living to Trinity College, Cambridge, in 1538, and there it remains.

Many of the church's priests have had less than peaceful ministries. In Henry IV's reign a Ware priest was hanged, drawn, and quartered for saying that Richard II was still alive. Another priest was a great horseman, and in 1476 is reputed to have ridden from Ware to St Michael's Mount, in Cornwall, and back in 20 consecutive days—an average of 32 miles a day.

In the 16th century several priests worked themselves into a theological lather over the beginnings of protestantism. In 1634 Isaac Craven was persecuted and ejected, in 1656 John Young was also ejected, but on a merrier note, Thomas Franklyn, vicar from 1759 to 77, officiated at the marriage of actor David Garrick.

Franklyn had been a Greek professor at Cambridge, and was made a Royal chaplain in 1767. A friend of Dr Johnson and Sir Joshua Reynolds, he was made chaplain to the Royal Academy. He moved from Ware to Brasted in 1777.

Greatest reformer was Joseph W. Blakesley, later Dean of Lincoln, who instigated the restoration of the church in 1849. He also stirred up the authorities over the condition of the houses in the poor parts of the town.

Another man with the right idea was John Trusler who lived between 1735 and 1820. In his early life this eccentric genius was curate at Ware. One of his more successful schemes was to send circulars to every parish in England and Ireland, saying he would print 150 sermons at 1s each to save the clergy both time and study. The plan worked.

It was Charles Chauncy (1592-1672) who probably had the stormiest passage of all. He was great-uncle to Sir Henry Chauncy, who wrote Hertfordshire's first history. Educated at Trinity College, Cambridge, he gained his BA in 1613 and his MA in 1617, following that up with a BD at Oxford. He became vicar of Ware in February 1627, and left in 1633. In 1630 he was before the High Commission Court for disregarding the oppressive measures of Archbishop Laud, and in 1635 he was there again for opposing the railing-in of the communion table at Ware.

He was suspended from office and thrown into prison. He only escaped by making a most humble apology, reading his submission to Laud's decrees on bended knee. But he never forgave himself, and, in 1637, he went to America. Laud described him as 'a most religious man who fled to New England for the sake of a good conscience.'

He became minister of Scituate, Mass., in 1641, but he was neither happy nor successful there. His congregation did not like their winter-born infants baptised in ice cold water, and everyone grumbled at another of his ideas, that the Lord's Supper must always be celebrated in the evening because the Last Supper occurred at that time of day. An invitation to return to Ware promised him, and his eight children, a comfortable retreat in his old age; and he was actually in Boston seeking passage for England when he was offered the presidency of Harvard University. He was by now 62, and had learned the lesson that there is a time to speak and a time to keep silent. He humbly accepted the new call, agreeing 'that he forbeare to disseminate or publish any Tenets concerning the necessity of immersion in Baptisme and Celebration of the Lord's Supper at Evening'.

No generation of Harvard students listened to so many sermons as the pupils of President Chauncy. His advice to former pupils when they took country parishes was excellent: 'Be plain preachers. Shoot not over the heads (and so over the hearts) of your hearers, like unskilful archers. Neither use any dark Latin words, or any derived thence, which poor people can't understand, without explaining of them, so that the poorest and simplest people may understand all.'

One of his sons, Isaac, born and baptised in Ware in 1632, went with his parents to America, where he studied theology and medicine at Harvard, and completed his education at Oxford. He became Rector of Woodborough, Wilts. He was ejected by the Act of Uniformity, and moved to the Congregational Church at Andover. From there he joined the College of Physicians, and then worked in London as a doctor. But in 1687 he accepted the pastorate of an independent meeting-house in St Mary, Axe. He was unpopular as a preacher, and a bigot, so his congregation left him. He later became divinity tutor of a Dissenting Academy in London, but died a year later in 1702.

His youngest brother, Israel, was one of the ten founders of Yale University on 16 October, 1701. He turned down the opportunity to be its first president, but served as Fellow (Trustee) until his death, in 1703, at the age of 59.

Another Ware vicar who figures in the Dictionary of National Biography is William Webster, the incumbent in 1740. He was a prolific writer on theological subjects. He died in 1758.

An independent chapel was built in 1778 in what was known as Dead Lane—now Church Street. The first minister was William Godwin, author of *Political Justice*. He stayed for two years. The chapel was eventually closed in 1918, when the organ was presented to the Methodist Church in New Road. The chapel building still stands, and is used as an auction room.

The United Reformed Church (formerly Congregational) just off High Street, was built in 1816 and rebuilt in 1856. At the latter date the extensive school buildings were built by Joseph Chuck, of Widbury House.

Christ Church was consecrated as the parish church of a new ecclesiastical parish on 9 November, 1858. The cost of founding the church was borne by Robert Hanbury who lived at Poles, which is just across the town boundary in the parish of Thundridge. He not only provided the land but also paid the cost of building the church and parsonage house and, later, a parish room and the original Christ Church Schools. He also built a mission hall in Amwell End in 1883. During the Queen Victoria Jubilee celebrations in 1887 a stained glass window—the East Window—was erected in his memory. He died in 1884. A stained glass window for the East End of the North Aisle was given in 1928 in memory of J. Chalmers-Hunt of Chadwell.

Both windows were destroyed in an air-raid in 1940 and fragments from both were used to make the West Window in 1948.

In that air-raid, on 18 September, a high explosive bomb dropped between the church and the vicarage, causing extensive damage to both buildings and also to the memorial hall and to the schools. Most of the windows of the church were destroyed and ceilings were brought down. There was also a hole in the roof. Until temporary repairs were completed, Sunday services were held in the school hall, not itself seriously affected.

Robert Hanbury was succeeded by his grandson Edmund Smith Hanbury, also a generous supporter of the church. He died in 1913. During that year the church tower was struck by lightning.

The Amwell End Mission Hall proved uphill work for Mr James Kinniburgh—a Scripture Reader—who took charge of it. Amwell End was not a pleasant quarter and contained a number of yards with somewhat insanitary houses. Twenty-four stood on the site of the present Drill Hall. E. S. Hanbury had that site and another in Baldock Street cleared, and re-housed the people in his model houses in Coronation Road.

After the 1914-18 war a memorial was erected to local members of the forces who had died. It consisted of a marble tablet bearing their names; carving was added to the communion table, and the carved oak reredos was built. It was a local effort. The stonemason was C. C. Smith, then a sidesman of the church; the oak was brought from the nearby Easneye Estate, and the carver was H. Gilbert, of West Street.

Long before the Welfare State, the Rev Alfred Oates, vicar from 1880 to 1914, developed a wide range of welfare and social services. Apart from financial help to hospitals and the running of day schools, the clergy and lay-workers organised clubs of various kinds. Clothing, coal and shoe clubs offered members bonuses to their contributions, and tradesmen gave a discount on goods bought with the club vouchers. The Penny Saving Bank encouraged thrift, and soup kitchens were opened in bad winters. The Children's Penny Dinner Fund was started in 1884, and children's breakfasts followed. The brass band flourished, but the choral society lasted only two years.

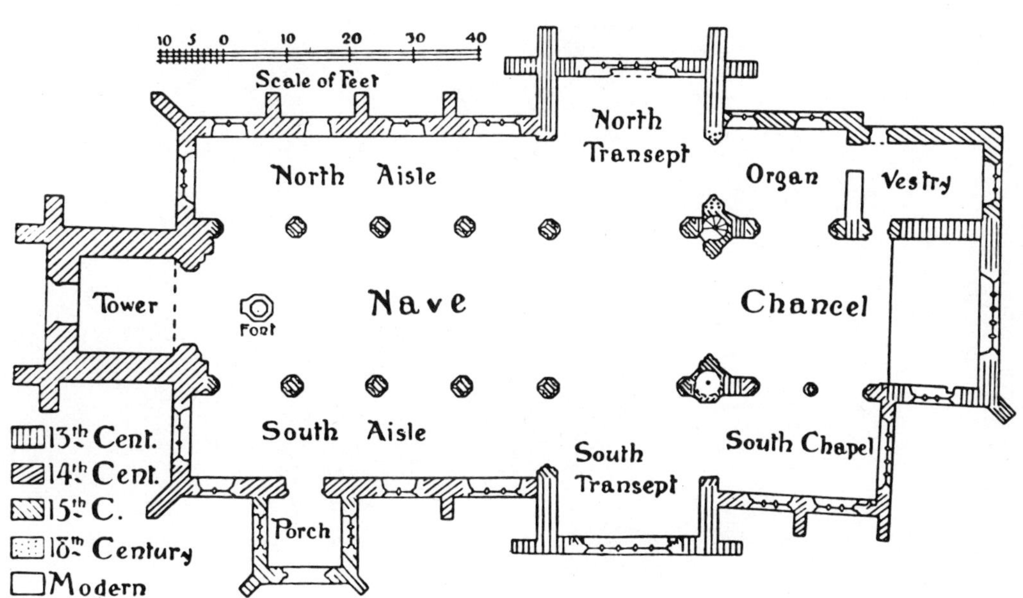

LEFT: St Mary's Church, 1854, about seven years after restoration, and RIGHT: Dean Blakesley, the Vicar of Ware responsible for the restoration.

BELOW: A plan of St Mary's showing the various sections and their dates.

ABOVE: The interior of St Mary's in 1868. LEFT: An early 19th century drawing of the font in St Mary's Church. Experts date it at 1380, but local tradition puts it at 1408. BELOW: St Mary's with the war memorial in the foreground. To the right is the old lock-up, now demolished.

LEFT: The Independent Chapel, founded in 1778 by William Godwin. It is now an auction room; RIGHT: A close-up of the date over the door.

BELOW: A print of Christ Church just after it was completed in 1858.

ABOVE: The Mission Hall in Amwell, built in 1883, and nearing demolition in March, 1958.

BELOW: The Catholic Apostolic Church at Ware in 1922.

LEFT: The Chantry, or cemetery chapel, in the early 19th century.

ABOVE RIGHT: The Methodist Church in New Road, and BELOW: The United Reformed Church was built in 1816, and rebuilt in 1856.

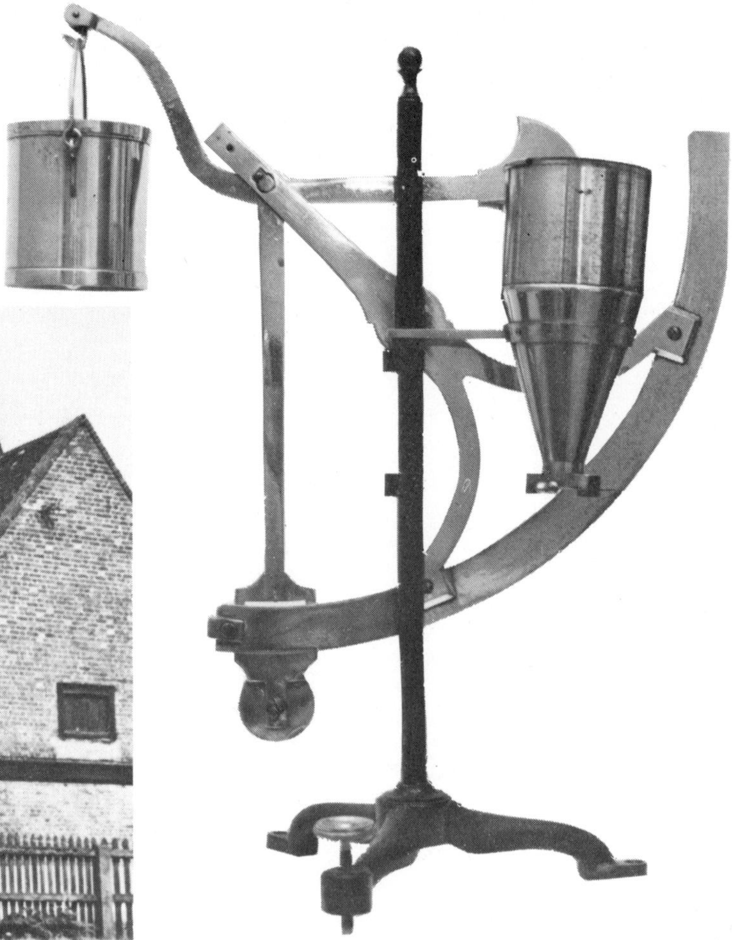

LEFT: Canons Malting, believed to have been built on what was part of the Alien Benedictine Priory's farm.

RIGHT: Late 19th century malting scales used in Ware.

BELOW: An industrial view of Ware from across the railway. In the centre is the factory of E. Dixon & Sons Ltd., millers and corn merchants.

The Compleat Trade

Thanks to its strategic position on road and river, Ware was from its early days a great malting town. How important it was can be gleaned from Pigot and Co's *Commercial Directory* of 1823-24: 'The principal trade is in malt and corn. Immense quantities of the former are conveyed to London; perhaps there is not a town in England in which more malting business is done.'

The Alien Benedictine monks made their own malt for brewing, and it is believed that the Canons maltings (named after a man named Canon), stand on the site of the original Benedictine building. Daniel Defoe, writing in 1724 mentions Ware as one of the towns 'from whence that vast quantity of malt, called Hertfordshire malt, is made which is esteemed the best in England.' At the time of Pigot's directory there were 22 maltsters in the town. All the buildings between the south side of High Street and the River Lee were once malthouses, and so were many others in the town.

A magnificent reminder of Ware's past is in Amwell End, where stand the Victoria Maltings, and adjoining buildings, owned at one time by Henry Page and Co. Ltd. Henry Page died in 1852; he had been in the malting trade for many years, as had his father before him, but it was his son who built up a relatively small local business into one of the foremost malting concerns in the country. The business is now owned by Pauls and Sandars.

The Ward family were also maltsters of repute. In the middle of the 18th century, Henry Ward started a malting business with a Mr Hudson, who in addition farmed at Noah's Ark Farm. In 1859 they owned four maltings, but by 1896 they had 18, some of which were in Hertford and Bishop's Stortford.

It was Isaac Walton who's ' Compleat Angler' indirectly gave Ware one of its biggest industries, Allen and Hanburys Ltd. William Ralph Dodd, who joined the firm at its home, Plough Court, in the City of London, in 1878, was an ardent fisherman, and vowed to fish wherever Isaac Walton had done so. In the autumn of 1895 he was fishing along the River Lee, and came upon the site of the old corn mills mentioned in the Domesday Book. There was still a derelict mill there, and old maps described it as Mill Mead. The New River Company owned the site, and the old mill buildings were adapted to Allen and Hanbury's needs. Part of Buryfield was acquired in 1898, and building has gone on apace as the firm has prospered, now stretching along Park Road.

The large red building in that area was designed and built in 1943 as one of the earliest factories for the large scale production of penicillin. However, the method for which it was designed became obsolete and it was adapted for other uses. The handsome building, in the angle of Park Road and Harris's Lane, houses most of the laboratories of Allen and Hanbury's Research Ltd.

The firm was founded at Plough Court, Lombard Street, in 1715 by Silvanus Bevan, an apothecary from Swansea. That remarkable Quaker, William Allen entered the business in 1792 and his son-in-law, Cornelius Hanbury I became a partner in 1822. The Hanburys of Hanbury in Worcestershire trace their history back to the 12th century when Roger de Hanbury held land in the neighbourhood. As was the custom then, the family derived its surname from their native place.

The firm's first expansion from Lombard Street was to a new factory at Bethnal Green in 1874, followed by the further expansion to Ware. The Ware site now accommodates the whole of the company's productive activities and also its research laboratories.

On the site of one of Ware's other Domesday mills stands the factory of Spillers French Milling Ltd., makers of Frenlite flour. The company, and its predecessors have occupied a premier position in the industry for more than 100 years.

About 90 years ago Dennis Wickham, member of a brewing family, but with a mechanical turn of mind, set up his own business making specialised machines for the brewing industry. D. Wickham and Co., was actually founded in 1886 as motor car and general engineers, having been appointed official repairers to the Royal Automobile Club. The first premises were in Priory Street, in what later became Ware Technical School.

When Dennis Wickham died in 1911, the business was carried on by his widow, with manager G. Henderson in charge of the works. By this time the motor car repair side had been dropped, and the main effort was concentrated on brewery machines and general engineering. There are still manhole covers about with the firm's name on them. The company had expanded by now into Viaduct Road, where it still is, but now it is known throughout the world as the manufacturer of diesel rail cars for passenger service. These run in many South American countries, in Jamaica, and in the Far East.

Industry in the town is diversified. Eastern Counties Farmers Ltd., have a large depot and mill in Star Street, and a newcomer is Rank's Precision Industries Ltd., in Watton Road. Furniture is made by Lurashell Ltd., and Wood Bros Ltd. (Old Charm) on the Marsh Lane industrial estate. Warecrete Products are also on the site. Further along, off London Road, Concrete Utilities is one of the major makers and suppliers of many of the lighting standards seen on our roads. This firm is actually in Gt Amwell parish, and it has an interesting museum of street lighting appliances.

ABOVE: On the site of one of Ware's Domesday mills—the flour mill owned by Spillers French Milling Ltd.

BELOW: The old corn stores in Star Lane, built about 1620 as a cavalry barracks.

An aerial view of the town sh
and Christ C

:s Lane maltings in the centre,
ight of them.

ABOVE: The Victoria Malting, owned by Paul and Sandars Ltd.

BELOW: Kiln House, No 16 Malting, Crib Street, in 1951.

Steps to be immediately taken in the case of Malt destroyed or damaged.

By the 7 & 8 Geo. 4, Cap. 52, Sec. 76, it is enacted that if any Malt shall be destroyed or damaged by Fire, or by the casting away of, or by any inevitable accident happening to, any Barge or Vessel in which such Malt shall be transporting or transported from one part to another of the United Kingdom, or on board, which such Malt shall have been put for that purpose, it shall be lawful for the Proprietor or Proprietors of the Malt to make proof of the accident, and cause thereof, on the Oath of one or more credible Witness or Witnesses, and of the Duty upon such Malt having been duly charged *and paid*, before the Justices of the Peace, at Quarter Sessions, for the County, Shire, Division, City, Town, or Place where such Malt shall have been made, or at, or next to the place where such accident shall have taken place or been first discovered, or where the Malt shall have been put on board, or before the Commissioners of Excise or any three of them*; and obtain relief according to the circumstances of the case, by strictly attending to, and following the directions contained in that Act, and the 11 Geo. 4, c. 17, s. 37, by which latter Act it is enacted that no person shall be entitled to any relief for any Malt destroyed or damaged—

Unless a Notice in Writing describing the Nature, Cause, and Extent of the accident, shall be delivered to the Commissioners of Excise, (now Commissioners of Inland Revenue) or Supervisor of the District in which such loss shall have taken place or been first discovered, *within Fourteen Days next after the same shall have come to the knowledge of the parties claiming relief.*

Nor unless they, or their Agent, shall also give Notice in Writing of their intention to apply for relief to the Collector or Supervisor of Excise of the Collection or District where the Quarter Sessions are to be held at which the application for relief is to be made, or to the Solicitor of Excise (now Inland Revenue) for England, when the application is intended to be made to the Commissioners, *Ten Days at least before the beginning of the Quarter Sessions, or before application to the Commissioners.*

Nor unless the application be made for relief *within Four Calendar Months after such accident shall have come to the knowledge of the party so applying.*

* For fuller Information as to the mode of proceeding after Notice of the loss is given, refer to the Act itself, 7 & 8 Geo. 4, c. 52, s. 76.

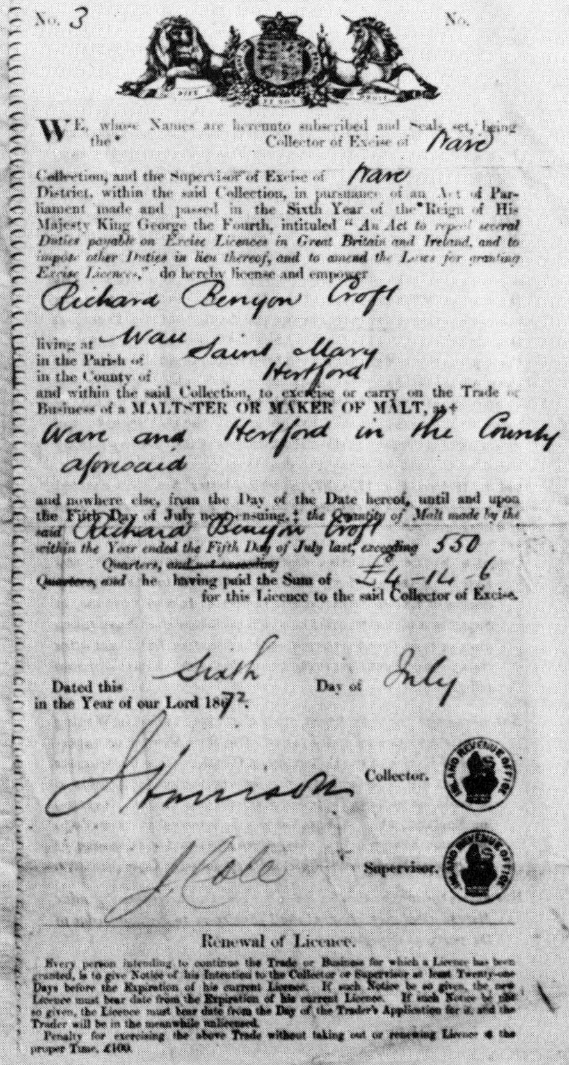

Maltster's Licence.—No. 315.

No. 3 No.

WE, whose Names are hereunto subscribed and Seals set, being the* Collector of Excise of Ware Collection, and the Supervisor of Excise of Ware District, within the said Collection, in pursuance of an Act of Parliament made and passed in the Sixth Year of the* Reign of His Majesty King George the Fourth, intituled "*An Act to repeal several Duties payable on Excise Licences in Great Britain and Ireland, and to impose other Duties in lieu thereof, and to amend the Laws for granting Excise Licences,*" do hereby license and empower Richard Benyon Croft living at Ware in the Parish of Saint Mary in the County of Hertford and within the said Collection, to exercise or carry on the Trade or Business of a MALTSTER OR MAKER OF MALT, at† Ware and Hertford in the County aforesaid and nowhere else, from the Day of the Date hereof, until and upon the Fifth Day of July next ensuing,‡ *the Quantity of Malt made by the said* Richard Benyon Croft *within the Year ended the Fifth Day of July last, exceeding* 550 *Quarters,* ~~*and not exceeding* Quarters,~~ *and* he having paid the Sum of £4-14-6 for this Licence to the said Collector of Excise.

Dated this Sixth Day of July in the Year of our Lord 1872.

J Harrison Collector.

J. Cole Supervisor.

Renewal of Licence.

Every person intending to continue the Trade or Business for which a Licence has been granted, is to give Notice of his Intention to the Collector or Supervisor at least Twenty-one Days before the Expiration of his current Licence. If such Notice be so given, the new Licence must bear date from the Expiration of his current Licence. If such Notice be not so given, the Licence must bear date from the Day of the Trader's Application for it, and the Trader will be in the meanwhile unlicensed.

Penalty for exercising the above Trade without taking out or renewing Licence at the proper Time, £100.

A Maltsters licence issued to Richard Benyon Croft in 1872.

LEFT: Cornelius Hanbury I (1796-1869), and RIGHT: William Ralph Dodd (1856-1917) who fished where Isaac Walton did, and in so doing found the site for Allen and Hanbury's Ware factory.

BELOW: On the site of the second Domesday mill, Ware Mill pictured in 1895 just before it was taken over by Allen and Hanbury's.

Bird's eye view of the Allen and Hanbury complex in 1950.

ABOVE: D. Wickham & Co., and CENTRE: a Wickham unit was made for the Jamaican Government Railways in 1951.

BELOW: Ware had its own bank at the beginning of the 19th century, and this £1 note is dated 1825. The bank went broke 25 years later.

LEFT: When D. Wickham & Co. opened, it made bottle filling machines like this.

RIGHT: The lamp post museum at Concrete Utilities.

ABOVE: Ware had its own gas works: the staff in the early 1920s.

BELOW: A lorry-borne Wickham train unit tries the tricky turn from Viaduct Road into Amwell End.

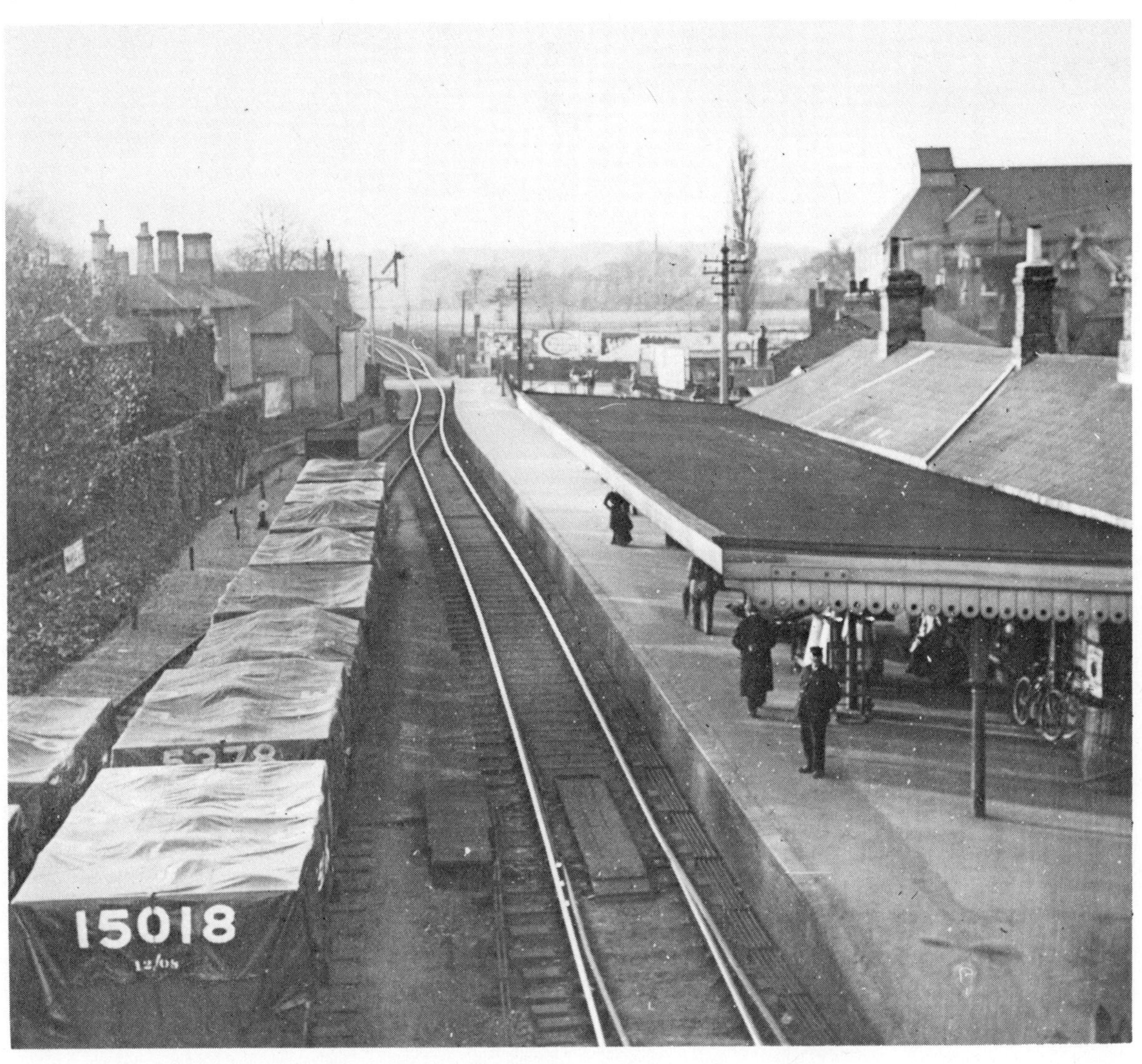

Ware station *c*1911.

The old Rose and Crown in Watton Road; a fine example of building with Caleb Hitch bricks.

Shooting Stars

On a dark night shooting stars light up the sky for a moment and they fade away. In the same way names appear in Ware's history for a brief moment and then disappear. We would like to know more about them, but the records take us no further.

One who did leave something of an autobiography was Friar Robert, a 13th century Ware man, who, to his family's despair joined the Franciscan Order when at Oxford. His story is told in a manuscript preserved in the library of the Honourable Society of Gray's Inn, London.

William of Ware was born in the 13th century, and joined the Franciscans. He became a renowned philosopher, and was in close touch with Duns Scotus, the great scholar of the time.

Whether Richard of Ware had anything to do with the town is difficult to say. That was his title when he first appears in history at Westminster in 1257. He became Abbot of that Benedictine establishment in 1258, and was made treasurer of England in 1283. He was the author of the 'Customary' which laid down the daily routine of the monastery. It included such instructions as 'Monks must shave each other, seniors first, because at the beginning razors are sharp and towels dry.' Bathing was restricted to four times a year. Linen nightcaps were permitted, but not scarlet or green or any other gaudy colour.

Thomas Fust was burned at the stake in Ware market place on 26 August, 1555. His offence? Speaking in an ill-advised and rude manner to Bishop Bonner.

The 16th century poet William Vallens was born at Ware and carried on business as a salter. Vallens' poem *The Tale of Two Swannes* is an early example of blank verse, and is a history of the River Lee, as Vallens calls it 'Ware-River'.

In the musical world, Simon Ive plays a part. Born in 1600, he was baptized in Ware on 20 July that year. He became lay-vicar of St Pauls, and at the restoration was installed eighth minor prebendary. He was chosen by Whitelock to co-operate with Henry and William Lawes in setting to music Shirley's masque *Triumph of Peace* and had many more works to his name.

What of Jane Stretton, daughter of Thomas Stretton, a wheelwright, who was baptised in St Mary's on 24 June, 1649? A pamphlet published in 1669 told the story of this unfortunate woman 'who hath been visited in a strange kind of manner by extraordinary and unusual fits, her abstaining from sustenance for the space of nine months, being haunted by Imps or Devils in the form of several Creatures here described. . . .'

She was reputed to have been put in that state by a 'Cunning Man' over the loss of a Bible. The wife of the man was brought to Jane after nine months, and she recovered enough to be able to take 'surrups' and such-like liquid ingredients.

Alexander Cruden, whose complete concordance of the Old and New Testaments is still a standard work, was born at Aberdeen in 1701, was intended for the Presbyterian ministry, but ill-health which for a time affected his mind, led him to take up teaching. For some time he was a private tutor in Ware until, in 1732 he opened a bookseller's shop in London. The Concordance was first published in 1736.

In about 1710 John Nickolls was born, son of a Quaker miller. He acquired the letters formerly owned by John Milton, which he published as *Original letters and papers of state addressed to Oliver Cromwell 1649-1658*. He collected 2,000 prints of heads from bookstalls around Moorfields, and furnished material for Joseph Ames's *Catalogue of English Heads*.

Caleb Hitch, born in 1785, died in 1851, was also a man worthy of mention, if only for his patent bricks, for which he had great hopes. The patent, granted in 1828, was not only for the bricks but for a wall composed of interlocking bricks.

He described his invention as having 'a wall built of bricks with hollows or cavaties in them, so formed that the whole work may be cemented together in one solid mass'. He claimed they would cost less to build, would need less mortar and have fewer joints. About 32 different types have been recorded, and, no doubt, the jigsaw involved puzzled both builder, trying to find out how many he would need, and bricklayer, who had to juggle with them. Examples of the bricks can still be seen in many parts of Ware and elsewhere.

Another Hitch, Nathaniel, was born in Ware on 31 May, 1845. He was the fourth son of George Hitch, a local builder. When he was quite a lad he attracted attention with a card model of St Mary's Church, and later he was apprenticed to stone and wood carving in London. He worked until he was 84, when he became blind, and he died in 1938 in his 93rd year. His best known works are figures and carvings in the cathedrals of Canterbury, Lincoln, Rochester, Norwich, Peterborough, Wells, Wakefield, and Truro; Calcutta, Sydney, Adelaide, and Newcastle (Australia). He handled restoration work at Westminster Hall, Hever Castle, and colleges at Cambridge and Oxford.

It is appropriate here to record one or two recent firsts: Cllr Charles Bowsher, for instance, who having been a previous chairman of Ware Urban Council, became the town's first Mayor at the change over of local government in 1974, and the following year, Mrs Elsie Barker who became the first woman mayor.

Then there were the gentlemen who took part in a duel in 1836. One was named Jones; the other was a jovial exciseman. The duel was staged in a saw-pit at Musley Dell. The exciseman fired into the air, whilst Jones dropped to the ground in fright.

He became even more terrified when he saw a red substance oozing from the exciseman's waistcoat—it was red currant jelly!

A sample of the interlocking bricks invented by Caleb Hitch (1785-1851).

ABOVE LEFT: William Palmer, first chairman of the Ware Board of Health 1849-1864, and BELOW: Mr S. P. Woollatt, first chairman of Ware Urban Council, 1894-1907.

ABOVE RIGHT: Mr Charles Bowsher, Ware's first Town Mayor, 1973/4, and BELOW: Mrs Elsie Barker, the first lady Town Mayor, 1974/75.

Great Amwell

The ecclesiastical parish of Great Amwell was, at one time, larger than most of the towns in the area. At the beginning of the 19th century Broxbourne was the southern boundary of the parish, and Hertford the western. It was only in 1976 that that part of Ware on the south bank of the River Lee was transferred to Christ Church, Ware. Evidence of Roman activity takes Great Amwell beyond recorded history—in 1847 urns and coins were found near the vicarage, which stands in the centre of a mound once known as Barrow or Burg Field.

How did it get its name? Most authorities agree that it was probably first Emma's Well, from the well which still exists below the church. But who was Emma? Legend says she was the wife of King Canute, and widow of Ethelred the Unready, but no one really knows. What we do know is that King Harold and Edward the Confessor were Lords of the Manor of Amwell.

Amwell has its place in history through Isaac Walton, who, in his book 'The Compleat Angler' made it the scene of his first fishing lesson. On Amwell-hill before sunrise, Piscator kept tryst with his friend Venator, and having merrily killed a bitch-otter and her helpless young, with the assistance of noble Mr Sadler's huntsmen and dogs, they adjourned to an honest alehouse, where they took a cup of good barley-wine, and sang 'Old Rose', before commencing the more serious business of the day, on the banks of the River Lee.

One of William the Conqueror's strongest supporters, Ralph de Limesi, held the manor at the time of Domesday Book. The same man founded Hertford Priory, and later became its Prior.

In the survey the manor was called Emmewelle, and it went on: 'It answered for fourteen hides and a half. There is land to sixteen ploughs. There are seven hides in the demesne, and there are two ploughs therein, and two more may be made.

'Twenty-four villanes with a priest and four foreigners, and seven bordars have there eight ploughs, and four may be made. There are nineteen cottagers and two bondmen; and one mill of six shillings. Meadow for sixteen ploughs. Pasture for the cattle of the village. Pennage for two hundred hogs; and for pasture and hay ten shillings. Its whole value is fourteen pounds and ten shillings; when received twelve pounds; in King Edward's time eighteen pounds. Earl Harold held this Manor.'

Amwell had a priest at the time of the Domesday survey, and the church was given by Ralph de Limesi to the Prior and Convent of St Mary at Hertford.

Later it came into the possession of the Abbot and Convent of St Peter, Westminster, and continued that way until the dissolution. Henry VIII gave it to Anthony Denny, a privy councillor, to whom the king also gave the Hertford Priory's property. He also owned Balls Park at Hertford—in 1086 within the Amwell manor. Sir Anthony later became Groom of the Stool.

By now the manor house was known as Amwellbury. It was purchased from the Denny family by Thomas Hobbes of Grey's Inn. The house now belongs to Sir John Hanbury.

The parish church, dedicated to St John the Baptist, has a lot in common with St Leonard's Church at Bengeo. The churches have Norman apses, two of only three in the county, and the ground plan of both churches is the same, the tower, vestry, and buttresses having been built later.

The tower is 15th century, and the church was restored, as was the fashion in 1866. There is a large brick mausoleum to the Mylne family at the church. Several generations of the family were engineers to the New River Company and one built the first Blackfriars Bridge in London.

There is a sarcophagus to Isaac Reed, who died in 1807. He was a Shakespearean commentator. Also buried at the church, but with no monument, was William Warner, a contemporary of Shakespeare. His most celebrated work was *Albion's England*—in which he traced British History in 13 books of verse. He translated into English Plautus's *Comedy of the Menaechmi*, which, it is said, gave Shakespeare the idea for *The Comedy of Errors*.

The man who had the biggest impact on Amwell was John Scott, the Quaker poet, born in Southwark on 9 January, 1730. He was a man who cultivated a taste for writing poetry, after being friendly with Charles Frogley, a bricklayer, and later John Turner of Ware. On his death, Dr Samuel Johnson, then near death himself, was prepared to write his biography, and this after Scott had written many critical pieces on the sayings and writings of Johnson. In a letter, Johnson wrote on 16 September 1784, 'As I have made some advances towards recovery, and loved Mr Scott, I am willing to do justice to his memory.' Alas the biography was never written. The notes were later given to John Hoole, translator, playwright, and glorified hack writer, a friend of both Johnson and Scott. His work is the only biographical book on Scott.

When the family moved to Amwell, to a house now part of Ware College of Further Education, and formerly Ware Grammar School, Scott went daily to Ware to a private school kept by a Mr. Hall. His teaching ability was mainly that of writing a clear hand, and the rudiments of penmanship. The family had a great fear of smallpox, however; it had been the main reason for moving from London, where his father had been a linen draper. This fear led him to be taken from the school, and the rest of his training was the result of self-discipline and the encouragement of better-educated friends.

It was Frogley who recognised the ability of Scott, and instilled in him a programme of intensive reading. Later Scott wrote *Ode XI To a Friend Apprehensive of Declining Friendship*—a poem which revealed Frogley's wistful speculation that his student would some day outgrow him.

Scott's father did well in the malting business at Amwell, but John's fear of smallpox kept him out of London. In fact, although he lived only 20 miles away, he only visited it once between 1740 and 1760.

It was not until he was 24 that his first verses were published. Turner and Frogley were responsible for this, urging on him caution before sending anything for publication. He wrote many poems, but it is generally agreed that his masterpiece is *Amwell*, which appeared in 1776.

Exactly when Scott started building his grotto is not quite clear, but the excavations were completed by the summer of 1773; legend has it that it cost him £10,000. It was well on its way, at least in Scott's mind, in the middle of the 1760s because Scott wrote to Turner, who was then in Exeter, asking him to gather shells and fossils for the work.

It was dug into a chalk hill in his garden, and by the time work on it was abandoned it consisted of seven chambers of various dimensions, all connected by passages, with walls covered with pebbles, ore, and fossils, all arranged in strange and curious patterns. On top of the hill, Scott built a summerhouse, which has no connection with the grotto.

In one chamber of the grotto, the ceiling is covered with white flint, and designs of a triangle, and two hearts and a crown have been created by black flints. The grotto extends 67 feet into the hill, and the lowest room is 34 feet below the surface of the earth. No one knows why he started it, but the popular belief is that it was a copy of one built by Alexander Pope at Twickenham.

The original visitor's book of the grotto is still held by Sir John Hanbury, and certainly many well-known figures of the period visited it. One of them was Dr Johnson, and it was a fashionable visiting place for London society on week-end excursions.

Even today, despite damage by vandals, the grotto attracts invited guests.

Scott wrote not only poetry, but anonymous pamphlets and essays, mostly political. He wrote a *Digest of the Highway and General Turnpike Laws*, and a series of critical essays. He married Charles Frogley's daughter, Sarah in 1767, but she died the following year in childbirth and their baby died some months later.

On 1 November 1770, he married Maria de Horne, and strangely enough it was while looking after her in London in 1783, that Scott himself died, at the age of 54. He was buried in the Quaker burial ground at Radcliff.

The original source of the New River marks out one of Great Amwell's most pleasant spots. Just above Emma's Well there is a spacious basin, and in the middle a small islet. In 1800, beneath weeping willows and other trees, architect Robert Mylne built a monumental pedestal to Sir Hugh Myddelton. Each side of the pedestal has a different inscription. On the small island is another pedestal with the following inscription:—

'Amwell, perpetual by thy stream
Nor e'er thy spring be less
Which thousands drink who never dream
Whence flows the boon they bless.
Too often thus ungrateful man
Blind and unconscious lives,
Enjoys kind Heaven's indulgent plan,
Nor thinks of Him who gives.'

The piece was written by Archdeacon Nares in 1818.

The churchyard too reveals some interesting 'poetry'. 'Here lieth the body of Mr Jeremiah Bennett, of this Parish, who departed this life 1st day of March, 1772, aged 38—Readers all, as you pass by; As you are now, so once was I; As I am now, so must you be: Prepare for death, and follow me.'

The verse on the tomb of Thomas Dorsett, died 28 May 1849, is not difficult to follow: 'Praises on tombs are vainly spent. A man's good deeds are his best monument.'

Ware from Amwell House garden, dated 1790.

ABOVE: Late 18th century print by Batty and Jukes of Great Amwell, showing women doing their washing in the New River.

BELOW: Pastoral scene in Great Amwell, 1800.

ABOVE: Late 18th century print of Amwell End, now part of Ware.

CENTRE: Amwellbury in 1827. The main building has been demolished; Sir John Hanbury's present home is on the right.

BELOW: An 1811 print of Amwell House, home of John Scott the Quaker Poet, now part of Ware College of Further Education.

ABOVE: Amwell House before the right wing was sliced off for road widening, and BELOW: The rear view.

ABOVE: The summer house of Scott's Amwell House, still in the grounds of Ware College.

BELOW: London Road, and the New River, pictured in 1920.

ABOVE: The George IV, Great Amwell, pictured in 1924.
BELOW: Pepper Hill, London Road, Great Amwell in 1920.

ABOVE: The original start of the New River at Great Amwell.

BELOW: The Wagon and Horses public house in 1892.

ABOVE: Building haystacks in 1894.

BELOW: St John the Baptist Church, 1793.

LEFT: Isaac Reed, a great Shakespearean commentator, buried in Gt. Amwell Church in 1807.

RIGHT: The Rev W. J. Harvey, Vicar of Gt. Amwell, who wrote a book 'Gt. Amwell past and present' in 1896.

BELOW: The interior of the Parish Church in 1893.

LEFT: Robert Mylne, one of a family of engineers who maintained the New River, and one of whom built the first Blackfriars Bridge in London.

RIGHT: The church from the New River in 1914.

BELOW: The chancel in the parish church. The tablet on the right is to William Duncan of the East India Company died March 14 1830, and on the left to Hannah Mylne (1836-1885).

MRS. LEICESTER'S SCHOOL.

DEDICATION.

TO THE

YOUNG LADIES AT AMWELL SCHOOL.

My dear young Friends,

THOUGH released from the business of the school, the absence of your governess confines me to Amwell during the vacation. I cannot better employ my leisure hours than in contributing to the amusement of you my kind pupils, who, by your affectionate attentions to my instructions, have rendered a life of labour pleasant to me.

On your return to school, I hope to have a fair copy ready to present to each of you, of your own biographical conversations last winter.

LEFT: Angel figures on a monument in the church.

RIGHT: A book entitled 'Mrs Leicester's School' was published in 1810. This is the dedication.

BELOW: A 15th century brass in the Parish Church, of a man and his two wives.

ABOVE: An interior picture of Scott's Grotto, and
BELOW: The entrance.

Two pages from the original visitor's book of Scott's Grotto. The entries on the first page are dated 1781, and on the second, 1785.

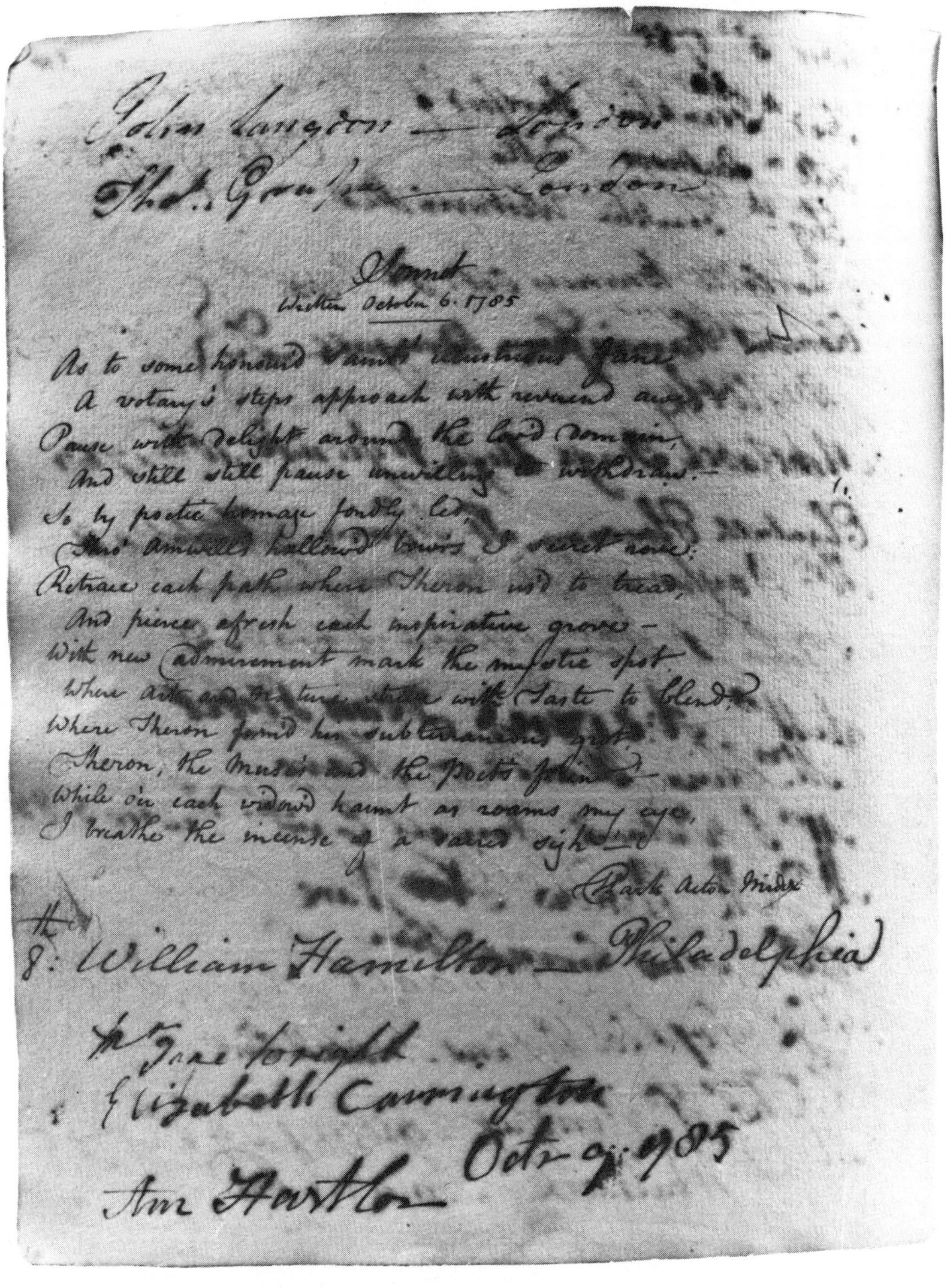

John Langdon — London
Thos. Grove — London

Sonnet
Written October 6. 1785

As to some honoured saint's illustrious fane
A votary's steps approach with reverend awe,
Pause with delight around the lov'd domain,
And still still pause unwilling to withdraw—
So by poetic homage fondly led,
Thro' Amwell's hallowed bowers I secret rove;
Retrace each path where Sheron us'd to tread,
And pierce afresh each inspirative grove—
With new admirement mark the majestic spot,
Where art and nature strive with Taste to blend,
Where Sheron form'd his subterraneous grot,
Sheron, the Muse's and the Poet's friend—
While in each widow'd haunt as roams my eye,
I breathe the incense of a sacred sigh—

Park Acton Midx

8th William Hamilton — Philadelphia

Mrs Jane Cartwright
Elizabeth Carrington
Octr 9. 1785
Ann Hartley

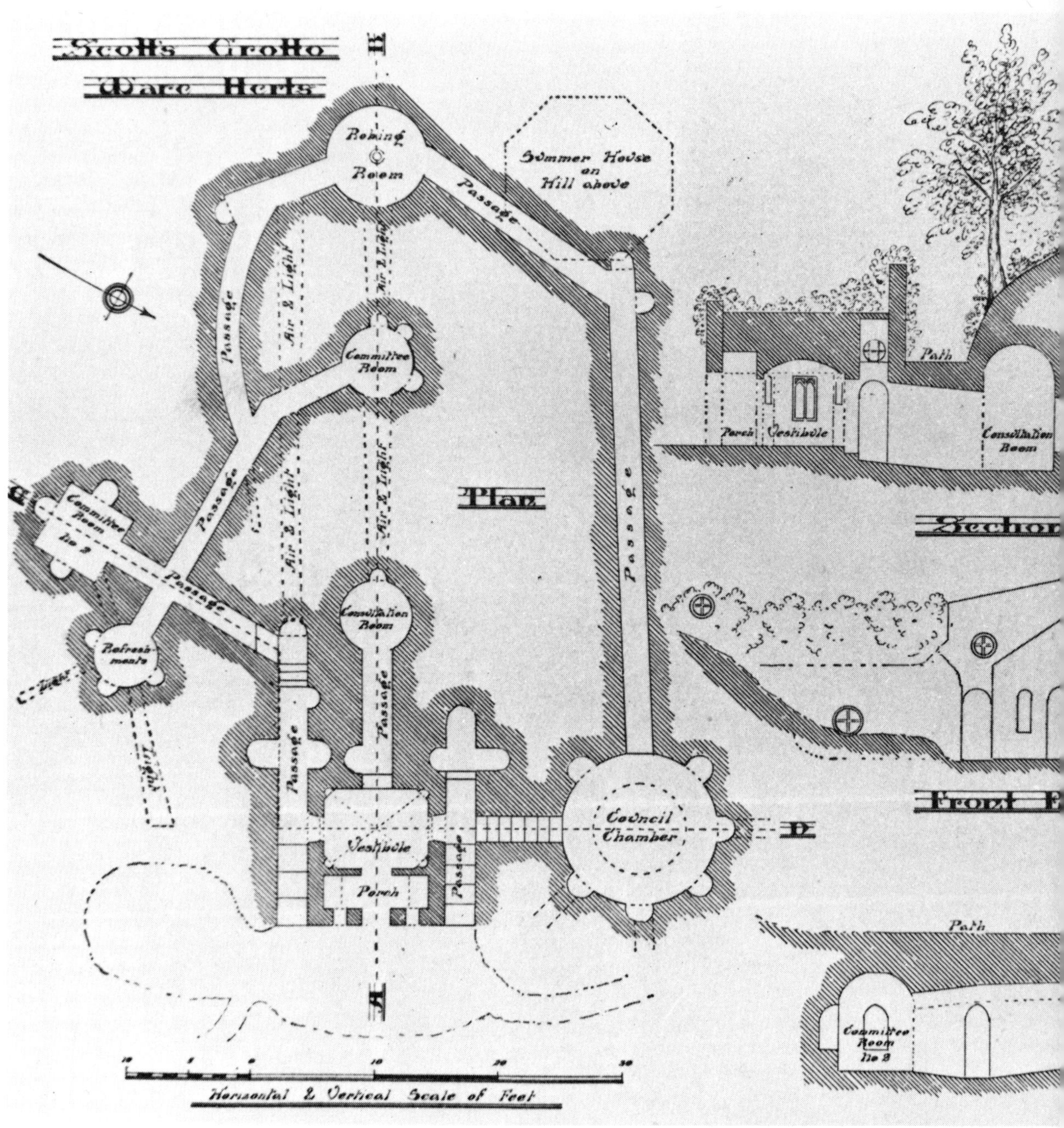

LEFT: A plan of Scott's grotto, drawn by Mr R. T. Andrews,

RIGHT: A fine pair of matched paintings. The first shows the ent the grotto, with John Scott sitting in a chair reading to the le picture. The second is the summer house, and a view of Ware fron garden.

Summer House
Committee Room
Air & Light
Robing Room
Council Chamber
C.D
R.T. Andrews, Survr
Hertford, Novr 1900

ABOVE: Ware celebrations held to mark the passing of the Reform Bill in 1832.

BELOW: The Post Office, Great Amwell, in 1916.

Vivat!

For a town that was nearly wiped out by a disastrous flood in 1408, Ware has survived to a remarkable degree. It is still interested in its past as fresh 'digs' turn up more of its Roman history, but it is also looking to the future as the exercise 'Vivat Ware!'—a joint venture for the enhancement of the town—awaits the right financial moment to take-off. It is to be hoped that, unlike so many ventures in other areas, it will not founder on the rocky shores of 'cost effectiveness'.

The coming of the railway in 1845 made it a commuting town, and until recently the town's High Street was choked with traffic, as the A10 spewed its heavy load of vehicles into the town.

This is now greatly reduced thanks to the opening in 1976 of the by-pass, which spans the Meads from the top of the former East Herts Golf course almost to Thundridge.

In 1973 the town was declared an 'outstanding conservation' area by the Historic Buildings Council, but that has not slowed down a rapid increase in house building on the periphery.

Generally speaking, the new has blended with the old. Many regretted the passing of the old Saracens Head public house, but the new one has opened up an attractive river frontage, from which barge trips can now be taken to Hertford.

Ware College of Education gives the town vitality, housed in new buildings, yet still retaining the home of John Scott, the Quaker poet. The house was formerly used by Ware Grammar School for Girls, but that school is now based at Presdales, former home of Mr Albert George Sandeman, of port fame.

Ware has not been well blessed with halls, although the Priory, formerly a private residence, has rooms for small ventures, and the Drill Hall, built for town use and not for the military, in 1899, is used for the big audiences attracted by the Ware Choral Society.

The society was founded in 1902, and except for a short break of three years during the 1939-45 war, it has kept good music alive in the town ever since. Over the years many soloists of international repute have sung with the choir.

The town also has a lively dramatic society started in 1947 as an evening institute class. It has won awards at Hertford Theatre Week on many occasions. An operatic society has recently been formed. The town band was started in 1895.

Ware is a caring town, and for 26 years it has had an active Old People's Welfare Association. In June, 1974 under its new name of Age Concern, a £32,000 Day Centre was opened in Priory Street.

The town has a thriving twin link with Wulfrath, in West Germany. Situated between the rivers Rhine, Ruhr and Wupper, that town is in the northern part of the former Duchy of Berg, dates to the 11th century, and is centered on lime production.

Ware, then, is a town of many surprises. To the motorist who passes through, and who only uses the main road, it is obviously an ancient town. But its many-sided facets are carefully hidden away.

For long threatened with an outsize relief road, Ware may now only have to contend with a less ambitious scheme to take traffic out of the main streets.

Because its industry is diversified, it can never quite suffer in the same way as a town which has all its industrial eggs in one basket.

It has a lively Chamber of Trade, and although it now only has a town council, it still has people who are prepared to make decisions which other towns shirk.

The fight to keep the car parks free of charge was an indication of this. This will to fight for recognition dates back to the days when it was overshadowed by Hertford.

That spirit is now so firmly implanted that no one, and no body is going to put Ware down.

Vivat Ware!

A view of Ware in 1841.

ABOVE: The Ware people knew how to enjoy themselves. This was High Street during the Queen Victoria Jubilee dinner in 1887.

BELOW: Presdales in 1859. The main house is part of Presdales School.

ABOVE: The Fire Brigade in 1912.

BELOW: King George V is proclaimed on May 18th 1910.

ABOVE: The High Street in 1908.

BELOW: Musley Infants School, which was formerly Ware Grammar School, and built as such.

ABOVE: The 1909 view from Scotts Road across Broadmead to the town.

BELOW: New Road in 1910.

High Street at the turn of the century.

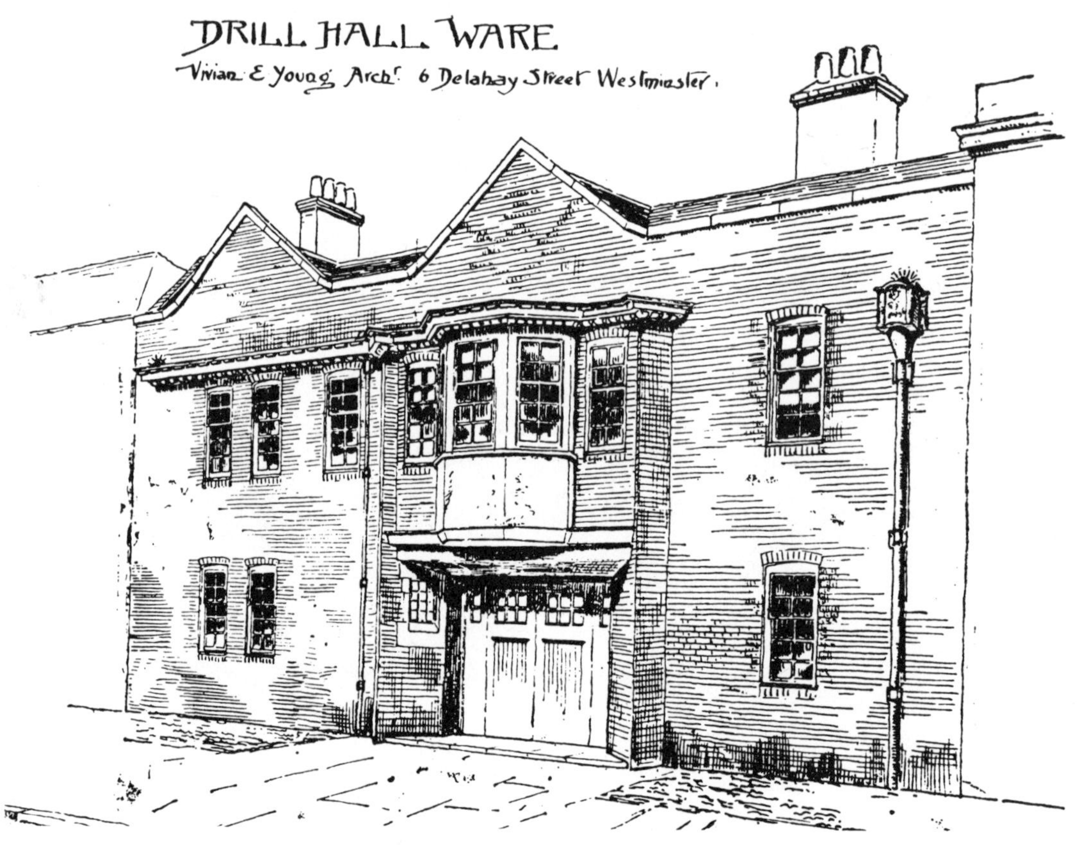

ABOVE: High Street—another view, *c*1900.

BELOW: *The Herts Guardian* announces the building of the Drill Hall in Amwell End, in 1899.

LEFT: The original Fanhams Hall, 1800. It was described in the Oldfield collection as Fathoms Hall.

RIGHT: In the 1940-1945 conflict, Lord Croft, (who was born at Fanhams Hall), was Under-Secretary of State for War.

BELOW: The dining room in the present Fanhams Hall, one of the town's social centres, and now part of the Building Societies Association.

ABOVE: The Queen Anne staircase in the original part of Fanhams Hall, and BELOW: The front of the house.

ABOVE: One of Ware's pleasure spots—the Japanese gardens at Fanhams Hall.

BELOW: High Street today, with its old coaching entrances.

West Street.

East Street.

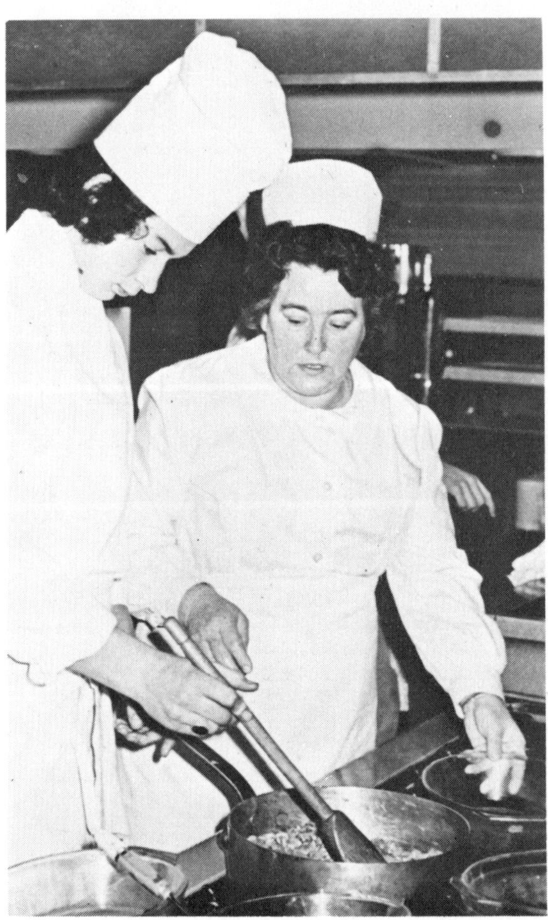

ABOVE: A general view of the new buildings at Ware College.

LEFT: Something cooking, and RIGHT: Engineering class at the College.

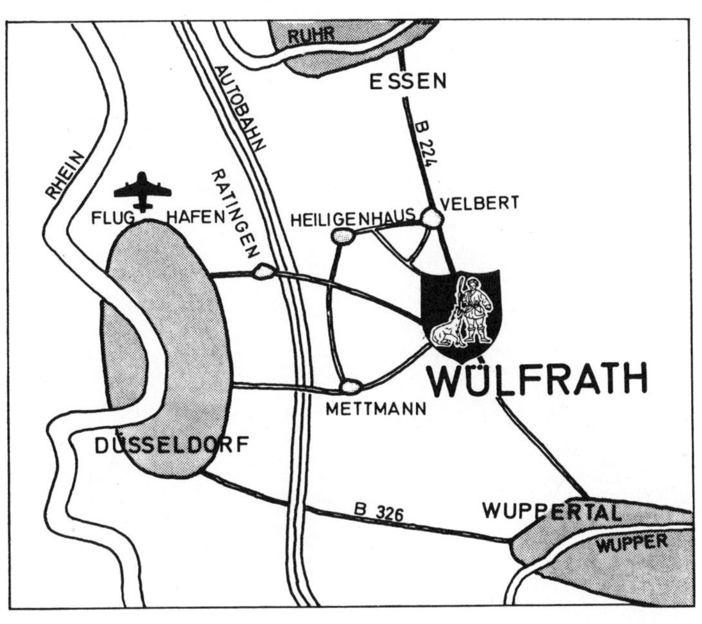

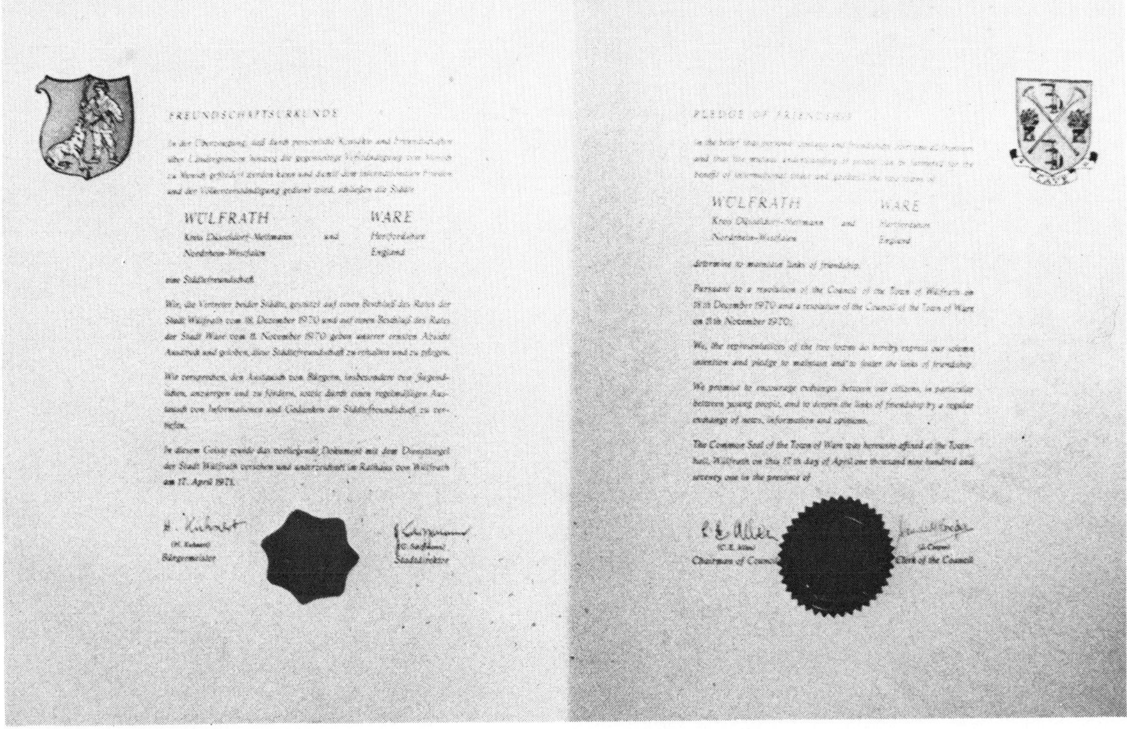

FREUNDSCHAFTSURKUNDE

In der Überzeugung, daß durch persönliche Kontakte und Freundschaften über Ländergrenzen hinweg die gegenseitige Verständigung von Mensch zu Mensch gefördert werden kann und damit dem internationalen Frieden und der Völkerverständigung gedient wird, schließen die Städte

WÜLFRATH, Kreis Düsseldorf-Mettmann, Nordrhein-Westfalen und WARE, Hertfordshire, England

eine Städtefreundschaft.

Wir, die Vertreter beider Städte, gestützt auf einen Beschluß des Rates der Stadt Wülfrath vom 18. Dezember 1970 und auf einen Beschluß des Rates der Stadt Ware vom 11. November 1970 geben unserer ernsten Absicht Ausdruck und geloben, diese Städtefreundschaft zu erhalten und zu pflegen.

Wir versprechen, den Austausch von Bürgern, insbesondere von Jugendlichen, anzuregen und zu fördern, sowie durch einen regelmäßigen Austausch von Informationen und Gedanken die Städtefreundschaft zu vertiefen.

In diesem Geiste wurde das vorliegende Dokument mit dem Dienstsiegel der Stadt Wülfrath versehen und unterzeichnet im Rathaus von Wülfrath am 17. April 1971.

([illegible]) Bürgermeister — ([illegible]) Stadtdirektor

PLEDGE OF FRIENDSHIP

In the belief that personal contacts and friendships between citizens and that the mutual understanding of people can be fostered for the benefit of international peace and goodwill, the two towns of

WÜLFRATH, Kreis Düsseldorf-Mettmann, Nordrhein-Westfalen and WARE, Hertfordshire, England

determine to maintain links of friendship.

Pursuant to a resolution of the Council of the Town of Wülfrath on 18th December 1970 and a resolution of the Council of the Town of Ware on 11th November 1970;

We, the representatives of the two towns do hereby express our solemn intention and pledge to maintain and to foster the links of friendship.

We promise to encourage exchanges between our citizens, in particular between young people, and to deepen the links of friendship by a regular exchange of news, information and opinions.

The Common Seal of the Town of Ware was hereunto affixed at the Town-hall, Wülfrath on this 17th day of April one thousand nine hundred and seventy one in the presence of

(C. E. Allen) Chairman of Council — ([illegible]) Clerk of the Council

ABOVE: A map of the Wulfrath area, Ware's twin-town, and BELOW: The twinning document.

WARE

UNDER THE

H. R. H. THE DU

CHARLES PHELIP

The RIGHT HON. The EARL

MOST NOBLE THE MARQUESS OF SALISBUR
RIGHT HON. THE EARL OF ESSEX,
RIGHT HON. EARL COWPER,
RIGHT HON. VISCOUNT MELBOURNE,
RIGHT HON. LORD JOHN TOWNSHEND,
LORD VISCOUNT FORDWICH,
LORD VISCOUNT GRIMSTONE,
RIGHT HON. LORD DACRE,
HON. AND REV. J. PEACHEY,
HON. AND REV. ROBERT EDEN,
RIGHT HON. SIR GORE OUSELEY, BART.
SIR J. SAUNDERS SEBRIGHT, BART. M. P.
SIR GEORGE DUCKETT, BART.
HON. BARON DIMSDALE,
ADMIRAL SIR D. GOULD, K. C. B.
SIR JAMES GAMBIER,
COLONEL WOOD, C. B.
ADMIRAL PEERE WILLIAMS FREEMAN,
ADMIRAL GOSSELIN,
REV. J. H. BATTEN, D. D.
REV. THOMAS LLOYD,
NICOLSON CALVERT, Esq. M. P.
THOMAS BYRON, Esq. M. P.

MARCHIONESS OF SALISBURY,
DOWAGER MARCHIONESS OF SALISBURY,
COUNTESS OF ESSEX,
COUNTESS COWPER,
COUNTESS OF VERULAM,
COUNTESS OF ATHLONE,
LADY JOHN TOWNSHEND,
LADY DACRE,
HON. MRS. EDEN,
HON. MRS. CALVERT,
LADY DUCKETT,
LADY OUSELEY,

HON. BARO
LADY GOUL
LADY GAMB
MRS. PHEL
MRS. PLUM
MRS. UNWI
MRS. WOOD
MRS. ORBY
MRS. BATT
MRS. BYRO
MRS. SMIT
MRS. A. SM
MRS. DICK

A Grand Selection

From the Works of HANDEL,

WILL BE PERFORM

On WEDNESDAY,

IN AID O

THE NATIONAL SCHOOL

Principal

MIS

MISS PALMER, A

MR.

MR. HAWES,

Principal Inst

LEADER OF THE

Messrs. MORALT, NICKS, LINDLEYS, R. ASHLEY, DAN
HARPER, PLATT,

CONDUCT

The Chorus will be selected from the King's Conce of the

FURTHER PARTICULAR

Doors will be opened at Eleven, and

A BALL AT THE TOW

LEFT: The old village church and surrounding timber houses in Wulfrath.

RIGHT: A splendid programme printed on silk for the Ware Festival in 1829. It was performed in St Mary's Church under the patronage of HRH The Duke of Gloucester.

VAL.

AGE OF

LOUCESTER,

the County,

Lieutenant of the County.

NGSBY DUNCOMBE, Esq. M. P.
TH, Esq. M. P.
, Esq. M. P.
IEETKERKE, Esq.
RGE THORNTON, Esq.
PE BYDE, Esq.
DICKINSON, Esq.
MER WARD, Esq.
S, Esq.
HEATHCOTE, Esq.
NBURY, Esq.
IELL, Esq.
STON, Esq.
, Esq.
COOK, Esq.
WN, Esq.
TOR, Esq.
N BULWER, Esq.
, Esq.
IBIER, Esq.
Esq.

MISS DICKINSON,
MRS. HADSLEY,
MISS HADSLEY,
MRS. DANIELL,
MRS. MEETKERKE,
MRS. WARE,
MRS. HANBURY,
MRS. COOK,
MRS. BROWN,
MRS. PARRY,
MRS. LLOYD,
MRS. GREEN.

ED MUSIC,

HOVEN, &c.

CHURCH,

26th, 1829,

IN CHARITIES:

MER,

S.

MER,

OKE, Jun. WILLMAN, MACKINTOSH,

ssisted by the Young Gentlemen

TIME.

at Twelve o'Clock.

EVENING,

PLAN OF THE PERFORMANCE.

PART I.

A Selection from Haydn's Creation.

Introduction . . (Chaos.)

Recitative . . . Mr. PHILLIPS,---"In the beginning."
Chorus . . . . . "And the Spirit of God."

Recitative . . . Mr. BRAHAM,---"And God saw."
Air . . . . and *Chorus*,---"Now vanish."

Recitative . . . Mr. PHILLIPS,---"And God made."
Air . . . . . . Miss M. CRAMER, and *Chorus*,---"The marvellous work."

Recitative . . . Mr. PHILLIPS,---"And God said."
Air . . . . "Rolling in foaming billows."

Recitative . . . Miss PATON,---"And God said, let the earth."
Air . . . . "With verdure clad."

Recitative . . . Mr. PHILLIPS,---"And the heavenly host."
Chorus . . . . . "Awake the harp."

Recitative . . . Mr. BRAHAM,---"And God said, let there."
Air . . . . "In splendour bright."

Grand Chorus . "The heavens are telling."
(The Soli parts by Miss M. CRAMER, Mr. BRAHAM, and Mr. PHILLIPS.)

Trio . . . . . . Miss PATON, Mr. BRAHAM and Mr. PHILLIPS, and *Chorus*,—
"Most beautiful appear."

Recitative . . . Miss PALMER,---"But who is He?" . . . . } *(Joshua)* *Handel.*
Air . . . . "Awful, pleasing Being." }

Anthem . . . . . "I was glad." (Composed for the Coronation of His Majesty.) *Attwood.*

*** *An interval of Ten Minutes between the First and Second Parts.*

PART II.

Voluntary, Organ, Mr. LUPPINO . . . . *Wesley.*

Air . . . . Mr. BRAHAM,---"O, liberty."
(Violoncello Obligato, Mr. LINDLEY.)

Trio . . . . . . Mr. HAWES, Mr. BRAHAM, & Mr. PHILLIPS,
and *Chorus*,---"Disdainful of danger."

Recitative . . . Miss PATON,---"O, let eternal honours."
Air . . . . "From mighty Kings."

Recitative . . . Mr. BRAHAM,---"My arms."
Air . . . . "Sound an alarm."
(Trumpet Obligato, Mr. HARPER.)

} *(Judas Maccabeus)* *Handel.*

Chorus . . . . . "We hear the pleasing, dreadful call."

Aria . . . . . . Miss M. CRAMER,---"Gratias agimus tibi." . . . . . . *Guglielmi.*
(Clarionet Obligato, Mr. WILLMAN.)

Recit. and Air . Mr. PHILLIPS,---"Angel of life." . . . . *Dr. Callcott.*
(Bassoon Obligato, Mr. MACKINTOSH.)

Chorus . . . . . "Rex tremendæ Majestatis." } *(Requiem)* *Mozart.*
Quartetto . . . . Miss M. CRAMER, Mr. HAWES, Mr. BRAHAM }
and Mr. PHILLIPS,---"Benedictus." }

Recitative . . . Miss PATON,---"Alas! I find." } *(Susanna)*
Air . . . . "If guiltless blood." }

Recitative . . . Mr. BRAHAM,---"O, loss of sight." } . . . . . *Handel.*
Air . . . . "Total eclipse." } *(Samson)*
Dead March . . }

Grand Chorus . "Hallelujah to the Father." *(Mount of Olives)* *Beethoven.*

H. BATTY, PRINTER, WARE.

One of the earliest purpose built cinemas in the area,
The Astoria, in Amwell End. Built about 1925.

ABOVE: Ware Town Band pictured in 1910 and CENTRE: Ware Dramatic Society's first full-length play was 'Acacia Avenue' presented in 1948.

BELOW: Ware Choral Society in a concert performance of 'Merrie England' in the 1934/35 season.

BACK COVER: John Gilpin on the way to Ware.

Bibliography

Wren Library, Trinity College, Cambridge. Box 44
Dictionary of National Biography
Chauncey's History of Hertfordshire
History of Ware by Mrs Edith Hunt
The Gerrish Collection, county archives
The Oldfield Collection, county archives
Vivat Ware! a policy document
My Life of Strife by Lord Croft
Through a City Archway—the story of Allen and Hanburys Ltd.
The Anglo-Saxon Chronicles
Cussan's History of Hertfordshire
Domesday Book
History of Gt Amwell by the Rev W. J. Harvey
Chronica Majora—Matthew Paris
Victoria County History
Herts During the Civil War by Alfred Kingston
Place Names of Hertfordshire—English Place Names Society
Lady Jane Grey by Hester W. Chapman
John Scott of Amwell by Lawrence D. Stewart
Principals of Harvard University—from the University

In addition there is considerable documentation in the county archives, the British Museum, and Hertford Museum which have been drawn upon.

Index

Subscribers

Presentation copies

1 Ware Town Council
2 East Herts District Council
3 Ware Library
4 Hertford Museum
5 Sir John Hanbury CBE
6 County Cllr. Charles Bowsher

7 Cyril Heath
8 Clive Birch
9 John & Marjorie Bishop
10 Martin & Elisabeth Barratt
11 Stephen J. Hantails
12 John Anthony Harrison
13 The Trinity School
14 Bridget B. Hantails
15 Ronald & Lesley Hutchings
16 Mr & Mrs C. W. Hemming
17 Dr & Mrs L. Leape
18 Herr Ullrich Scmiller, Burgomeister of Wülfrath
19 Miss J. M. Pamphilon
20 F. A. Hobbs
21 Mrs Rosemary Pollard
22 Mrs C. A. Baldwin
23 Mrs G. P. Norris
24 Mrs Peggy Murphy
25 Mrs S. P. Robbins
26 D. E. F. Perkins
27 Mrs E. H. Scott
28 Mr & Mrs N. Sanders
29 Mrs V. J. Crown
30 Miss Angela Smedley
31 Mrs S. A. Murley
32 Mrs V. Urwin
33 Miss D. J. Gilbert
34 C. W. Hughes
35 Mr & Mrs T. J. Page
36 R. W. Jenkins
37 A. M. Wiggall
38 Miss B. A. Wilbourn
39 Mrs J. M. Cable
40 Mrs P. A. Carpenter
41 T. C. Corby
42 Mrs S. R. Watts
43 Mr Capel
44 Miss Christina Martin
45 Mrs M. J. Darling
46 Mrs D. A. Wade
47 Mrs B. M. Rosser
48 Mrs Lois A. Harris
49 N. D. A. Murkin
50 Mrs E. K. Samways
51 W. G. Sangster
52 Miss R. J. Murkin
53 Mrs M. D. Branch
54 D. A. Bardwell
55 C. A. Bardwell
56 P. C. Margle
57 M. F. Collins
58 Mrs M. Stevens
59 J. M. Barnes
60 Mrs Etta Van Dyck
61 Mrs A. I. Powell
62–67 Herts County Library
68 Stephen & Linda Nendick
69–78 Ware Library
79 Mr & Mrs Gladding
80–87 Ware Library
88–127 Bibliographical Unit, East Divisional H.Q., Stevenage
128 K. G. & R. M. C. Weeks
129 Mr & Mrs D. Donoghue
130 Mr & Mrs F. C. Bevan
131 Mr & Mrs D. R. Robertson
132 Mr & Mrs M. G. Conlon
133 W. G. Thomas
134 Mr & Mrs G. F. Bailey
135 R. E. Parker
136 D. G. A. Myall
137 Mr & Mrs J. B. Chadwick
138 Ruth & David Freeman
139 Barbara & Arthur Maiden
140 Miss S. Donoghue
141 R. H. Owen
142 Lin & Charles Pearce
143 B. Laws
144 Graham H. Tritt
145 B. J. Gravestock
146 Mr & Mrs E. Chase
147 Mr & Mrs D. Easter
148 Mr & Mrs W. J. Hewitt
149 Mr & Mrs R. E. Dean
150 J. A. Bell
151 Mr & Mrs J. W. J. Marshall
152 D. A. Gray
153 The Wright Family
154 Dr C. R. Pick
155 C. H. Dod
156 Alan L. Warman
157 J. H. J. Tapper
158 Mrs G. Howarth
159 Mrs J. Yates
160 Mrs S. McEwen
161 Miss J. M. Richardson
162 Miss G. Clark
163 Mrs E. D. Jennings
164 Mr & Mrs D. A. Butcher
165 St Catherine's JMI School
166 Mrs P. Daniels
167 Mrs K. Crisp
168 Mr & Mrs S. A. Goodlew
169 L. S. Beeston
170 Mrs E. W. Rowell
171 Mrs R. V. Swann
172 Mrs B. N. Sprules
173 Mr & Mrs H. J. Page
174 Fred & Rosemary Pope
175 Mr & Mrs J. Kubista
176 Mr & Mrs R. H. Kay
177 Mr & Mrs B. Stockwell
178 Mr & Mrs R. Andrews
179 Mr & Mrs R. Way
180 Mr & Mrs M. B. McAleer
181 Mr & Mrs D. J. Papper
182 Miss E. Hankin
183 Miss J. Pollard
184 Mrs M. Stockman
185 Mrs Marion Rouse
186 I. Brown
187 Miss M. M. R. Stewart
188 Mrs M. Davis
189 Mrs J. M. Alexander
190 Mrs Dyson
191 Mrs V. Hillier
192 P. K. Geer
193 Mrs B. Morris
194 Mrs R. A. Smart
195 R. D. Tarling
196 Mr & Mrs R. A. Oswald
197 Mrs R. Penn
198 Michael G. Ottley
199 Mrs B. A. Smith
200 Josette K. M. Koenig
201 Michael Waller
202 B. D. Hudson
203 C. F. Best
204 M. J. Wills
205 Suzanne Vernon
206 G. S. Janes
207 A. J. Wright
208 R. L. Kench
209 Richard Grahame Williams
210 Dr J. E. Moore
211 Miss J. M. Freeman
212 Mrs J. Freeman
213 S. Cadmore
214 Dr J. M. W. Sedgwick
215 J. T. Baker, BEM
216 Mrs V. M. Prince
217 D. F. Salter
218 F. W. Woodhouse
219 Mr & Mrs A. Newman
220 S. Baldock
221 Mrs P. M. Bays
222 Mrs B. Eatenton
223 Mrs P. A. Frank
224 Mrs A. Thurgood
225 Peter Rolfe
226 G. V. Kenyon
227 Mrs S. J. Timms
228 Mrs B. Davies
229 Mrs O. G. Cannon
230 Mrs W. H. T. Hart
231 G. B. Herriott
232 The Trinity School Library
233 Miss J. Williams
234 T. W. Platten
235 The County Records Office
236 Mrs M. Myddleton
237 Janet Phipps
238 Hugh C. Weller-Lewis
239 Mrs V. Johnson
240 Richard C. Andrews
241 Paul E. Damen
242 John A. G. Royce
243 Ann P. Redding
244 Mrs E. K. Best
245 Peter John Fordham

246 Mr & Mrs Raymond John Wright
247 R. I. Murray
248 Miss Dorothy Charvill
249 Miss M. A. Tillcock
250 Miss Sandra Jolly
251 R. A. Sissens
252 Miss Vanessa St. Margaret Moore
253 Mrs D. Breckon
254 Mrs S. Pike
255 Mrs P. Chapman
256 T. Meadows
257 Mrs E. Jordan
258 Miss M. Meggy
259 Mrs Maureen Johnson
260 Mrs S. Y. Garrett
261 R. G. Stevens
262 F. E. Ridley
263 A. Chalmers
264 D. J. Adams
265 H. Harwood
266 E. Dives
267 Miss V. G. Hamilton
268 Mrs A. Gay
269 Miss O. A. Lambert
270 H. F. Patston
271 A. M. Hickling
272 R. C. Perkins
273 Ursula S. Büttner
274 Mrs F. A. Cutts
275 A. J. Heil
276 David Samuel Hannaford
277 Dr R. A. Hardie
278 C. Y. Hardie
279 R. J. Norton
280 Mrs J. Graham
281 J. R. Mayoss
282 The Revd Hugh E. Wilcox
283 Mrs M. R. Sims
284 F. Arnold
285 C. A. Smith
286 P. C. Tyser
287 G. Gull
288 Mrs E. Proctor
289 Mrs Patricia Hart
290 Rev John Bournon
291 John Budworth
292 Hoddesdon Library
293 Mrs J. Clifton
294 Mrs Brain
295 Mrs M. E. Munt
296 Mrs L. Faircloth
297 Miss Sally Robinson
298 Mrs M. R. Gerrard
299 Miss Fiona M. Sims
300 Helen M. Sims
301 W. Brunton
302 Mrs J. A. Grieves
303 V. R. Gray
304 C. R. Hissey
305 R. A. Hackett
306–315 Mrs Charles Arthur Ware
316 R. J. Munt
317 M. High
318 J. L. Wright
319 V. Hart
320 P. M. Davies
321 Mr Timmons
322 Mrs J. R. Case
323 Mrs A. M. Powers
324 C. O. Harrison
325 H. Oldham Smith
326 Mr & Mrs J. R. Knight
327 Mrs Katrina Vine
328 Lloyds Bank Ltd
329 R. R. Bouttell
330 N. Murphy
331 Mrs G. M. Burdett
332 Mrs V. Willer
333 Mrs L. Tebbutt
334 Lesley Swan
335 Mrs O. Burgess
336 Mrs I. M. Fleetwood
337 Mrs Pearl Holloran
338 E. C. Allen
339 I. B. M. Darby
340 Mrs J. G. Grose
341 Mrs A. Campkin
342 R. A. Moore
343 D. H. Boltwood
344 Mrs J. Adams
345 Kenneth John Ives
346 L. A. Smith
347 Mrs M. L. Riches
348 Mrs D. E. Newell
349 P. W. Parker
350 Julian L. A. Kerrell-Vaughan
351 Miss L. M. Badcock
352 Mrs J. D. Lloyd
353 A. E. Spicer
354 F. Todd
355 G. M. Read
356 Mrs P. C. Hart
357 Herr H. Küpper
358 D. Maddams
359 F. J. Brown
360 R. W. Wells
361 C. Willsher
362 Mr & Mrs A. Jones
363 Richard Shackle
364 J. H. Hatfield
365 Mrs D. Pearce
366 Mrs B. Martin
367 A. Moulsdale
368 Mrs S. E. Carr
369 D. G. Barr
370 D. I. Andrews
371 Mr & Mrs Reid Winter
372 Mrs Z. Marshall
373 Mrs V. Nelson
374 Bernard Carter
375 Mr & Mrs J. A. Broom
376 T. W. Hills
377 A. Lester
378 W. Taylor
379 Mr Pegrum
380 C. W. Dennis
381 A. R. Kingsnorth
382 T. V. Bacon
383 E. Moult
384 Miss M. M. Goldstone
385 Mrs H. F. Bayford
386 W. J. Fulwell
387 Miss A. F. Jones
388 Mrs C. Blackmore
389 Mrs N. F. Webb
390 M. F. Kensey
391 Miss T. Svenson
392 Hans Gibhard Bott
393 Frank Goodey
394 B. V. Ball
395–396 M. Dorrington
397 J. L. Craigs
398 R. K. Brookfield
399 A. J. Lloyd
400 Mrs B. J. Reed
401 Mrs A. Phelps
402 Mr & Mrs Wm Hansing
403 K. Birkenbaums
404 Miss U. J. Barnard
405 A. E. Surridge
406 G. Sayers
407 John C. Pavey
408 Mr & Mrs W. Ruskin
409 R. G. Stabler
410 Mrs R. Reeves
411 Mrs B. Beeson
412 Mr & Mrs D. Prior
413 H. Pasfield
414 Mr & Mrs A. J. Horne
415 J. Easter
416 A. D. Spence
417 Mr & Mrs B. Fry
418 Mrs R. J. Huggins
419 A. Browne
420 Christopher Andrew Hall
421 Mrs J. H. Carver
422 R. A. K. Radford
423 R. Kenway
424 Mrs L. Wallace
425 Mr & Mrs R. Benfield
426 B. Taylor
427 Mrs J. Wiffen
428 Mrs E. Pateman
429 Dr J. M. Ferrar
430 Mrs Allard
431 Mrs A. P. Osborne
432 R. Argent
433 Mrs D. Morris
434 Derek M. Smith
435 Mrs J. D. Goodey
436 Mrs L. Wallace
437 A. C. Turner
438 Mrs S. L. Steed
439 J. Gilbert
440 Mrs D. B. Bethell
441 R. W. Jones
442 Mrs J. Gilby
443 Mrs M. A. Curd
444 B. Jones
445 Miss M. Jones
446 A. L. Rear
447 Mrs E. Page
448 R. J. W. Freeman
449 Mrs E. Mellish
450 L. M. Suckling
451 Mrs P. M. Harwood
452 Rowland, Nevill & Co.
453–454 Mrs Bateman
455 C. MacDonald
456 Mrs D. R. Pilliner
457 E. Poyser
458 Mrs M. E. Watson
459 Mrs H. Cruse
460 Mrs M. Harwood
461 Mrs A. Wilbourne
462 J. D. Evans
463 Mrs L. McNeil
464 V. Webb
465 R. L. Blakes
466 Mr & Mrs O. Singletary
467 R. Page Croft
468 Donna Pumfrey
469 Lt Cdr Mrs Jerald B. Anderson
470 Reg & Dora Davey
471 Mrs Olive Gray
472 A. J. Vigus
473 Mr & Mrs G. Lewis
474 Mrs J. Reynolds
475 J. Maurice Edwards
476 Jacqueline E. Davison
477 G. S. Gibbs
478 Mr & Mrs D. Rhodes
479 Mr & Mrs P. G. Hodges
480 Margaret M. Morris
481 S. G. Wright
482 Mrs S. Smith
483 Mr & Mrs S. G. Perkins
484 W. H. Christie
485 John Michael Hunt
486 Jonathan L. Wells
487 Miss M. J. Reid
488 Mrs K. Watmough
489 Ivy Morgan
490 John Gosbee
491–492 The County Archivist
493 Mr & Mrs A. S. Hawdon
494 B. W. Smith
495 Peter Ruffles
496 M. J. & F. S. Stevenson
497 Eileen Lynch
498 Jennifer A. Gray
499 Mrs E. M. Oakley
500 Charles William Hulls
501 Miss A. K. Frary
502 Christopher F. Mulcahy
503 Mrs Judith Anne Wyles
504 Mrs I. E. Gray
505 B. W. Parrott
506 Marian Newton
507 Mrs E. Nix
508 Mr & Mrs R. L. Helmore
509 Mrs I. J. Hopkins
510 E. N. Long
511 E. A. J. Mansfield
512 Mrs N. Wells
513 Mrs D. A. Stanbridge
514 Mrs V. Chappel
515 R. J. A. Wakely
516 E. A. Lanaway
517 P. G. T. Fogg
518 Mrs J. Drury
519 J. Fletcher
520 D. A. Storey
521–522 Dr C. P. Fellows
523 A. G. Baker
524 Mrs P. A. Green
525 Terence Hards
526 Michael & Barbara David
527 L. J. Greer
528 Miss M. D. Worrim
529 Mr Adams
530 Mr & Mrs Portmock
531 L. Jarvis

532 Paul Damen
533 Mike Poultney
534 G. W. May
535 A. Nimmo
536 Mrs D. R. Pilliner
537 May Avery
538 S. G. Woods
539 Brian Smith
540 D. T. Hyatt
541 M. Light
542 Mr & Mrs Paul Ingle
543 Edward T. Booth
544 The Bishop of Hertford
545 Mike Glue
546 C. B. Uershaw
547 Mr & Mrs D. Golding
548 Mr & Mrs R. Collyns
549 Anne, Roy, Celia and Jeffrey
550 Mrs D. M. Bennett
551 Stephen Bennett
552 A. V. Pedder
553 D. A. Moore
554 Mrs B. R. Wallis
555 Chris Dunn
556 Mrs K. Clarke
557 Ian D. McWeeney
558 Nigel J. Hatherly
559 George Kilsby
560, 561 Miss J. Dale
562 Mrs Marilyn Anne Botheras
563 C. A. S. Melton
564 Mrs K. Mears
565 Miss Deborah Stringer
566 P. E. Hutton
567 J. A. Game
568 R. J. Lloyd
569 David Smith
570 Mrs I. R. Glassett
571 H. F. Eastman
572 B. Porter
573 Donald William Slater
574 G. R. Williams
575, 576 Joan Pallett
577 E. F. Wilbourne
578 L. C. Pratt
579 R. A. Burr
580 C. S. Leatherland
581 Mrs C. L. Grove
582 Victoria Sugrue
583 C. Scales
584 Mrs A. M. Knowles
585 Mr Trundell
586 Frank L. Hibberd
587 William Maskell
588 D. Brand
589 J. C. Miller
590 H. Wilbourn
591 Frederick G. Milton
592 D. J. Mills
593 D. H. Donoghue
594 R. W. Page
595, 596 A. Stockwell
597 Mrs B. W. Wadey
598 Keith F. Parrott
599 Frederick Arthur French
600 P. W. Todd
601 G. Littlechild
602 Rev C. E. C. Walker
603 Mrs C. Wood
604 David Perman
605 Mrs B. M. Marshall
606 Haileybury and Imperial Service College
607 W. J. M. Lea
608 J. & R. M. Adams
609 Mr & Mrs D. Washbrook
610 Peter R. Bonfield
611 D. S. Clark
612 J. W. Underwood
613 D. R. Atkins
614 R. R. Trimby
615 Michael T. Saggers
616 Anne Barr
617 V. E. C. Devonshire
618 D. Page
619 Michael Sheppard
620 Mrs Gray
621 F. Vincent
622 Mrs Beryl Rawlinson
623 T. W. Gladwin
624 Charles Clift
625 J. A. Platt
626 Mrs J. Boxall
627 John Michael Evans
628 Mrs I. M. Harris
629 J. Spearman
630 Cathy Ives
631 M. J. Turner
632 V. C. Knight
633 I. E. Murton
634 K. J. & J. A. Campbell
635 D. W. Day
636 Dennis J. Clark
637 Miss Margaret G. Pritchard
638, 639 Mrs Susan Batty
640 Elizabeth Wells
641 G. C. Metcalf
642 W. Rist
643 Mr & Mrs H. Turner
644 M. M. Burnie
645 Pauls and Sandars Ltd.
646 Mrs P. Warner
647 Alfred W. Hanmore
648 J. Michaels
649 K. W. Wood
650 Mrs L. R. Stevenson
651 Mrs K. M. Leskovych
652 J. A. Goodrick
653 H. Taylor
654 Mrs P. Brace
655 P. Robinson
656 T. Jones
657 Miss M. Jones
658 D. Taylor
659 Mrs K. Dennett
660 Mrs J. Wildman
661 Jean Christine Indge
662 Bobbie Ward
663 Jack D. Garratt
664 Margaret Smart
665 S. F. Ellender
666 David Brittain
667 Jacqueline Fisher
668 R. E. Day
669 George B. Sapsford, FCA
670 Edward Sapstead
671 Thomas Smith
672 H. M. Hoather
673 Mr & Mrs D. L. Hoy
674 A. M. Foster
675 Matthew Self
676 T. J. Beardsmore
677 Mrs Margaret Pinder
678 Zena Newell
679 Mrs J. Stevens
680 Cyril John James
681 The Ware Society
682 Mrs M. E. Cottle
683 D. A. Hawkes
684 Peter Chard
685 Malcolm Read
686 David Read
687 F. R. Smith
688 Stephen & Vicki Wegg-Prosser
689 John Walker
690 Valerie C. Baskwill
691 J. R. Alcock
692 T. Kitchener
693 Stadt Wülfrath
694 Mrs M. A. Rooke
695 Mrs A. Knight
696–699 East Herts School Library Service
700, 701 School Library Service HQ
702 Brian C. Lee
703 Clifford Longman
704, 705 Mid Herts School Library Service
706 E. J. Stevens
707 S. & R. Burgess
708 E. N. Clegg
709 Timothy I. Hantails
710 Joan & Tony Lammiman

Remaining names unlisted.

ENDPAPERS: FRONT—Plan of the Priory (it was really a Friary) when it was offered for sale as a private estate in 1906.

BACK—A dramatic picture of the centre of Ware taken in 1976 from a hot air balloon. Pilot and photographer was Mike Glue. To the left of the church is the building now known as The Manor, but it is a survival of the mediaeval priory.